MIKE HAILWOOD

MIKE HAILWOOD

A MOTORCYCLE RACING LEGEND

MICK WOOLLETT

Foreword by Giacomo Agostini

Haynes Publishing

Dedication
To my wife Peta and
our three children, Joanne, Paul and Guy,
who saw very little of me during the spring,
summer and autumn weekends when
Mike the Bike reigned supreme.

First published April 2000

British Library Cataloguing in Publication Data:
A catalogue record for this book is available from the British Library

ISBN 1 85960 648 2

Library of Congress catalog card no. 99-73263

Haynes North America Inc.,
861 Lawrence Drive, Newbury Park, California 91320, USA.

Published by Haynes Publishing,
Sparkford, Nr Yeovil, Somerset BA22 7JJ.

Tel: 01963 440635 Fax: 01963 440001
Int.tel: +44 1963 440635 Int fax: +44 1963 440001

E-mail: sales@haynes-manuals.co.uk
Web site: www.haynes.co.uk

Designed and typeset by G&M, Raunds, Northamptonshire
Printed and bound in Great Britain by J. H. Haynes & Co. Ltd

Endpapers
Front: Giacomo Agostini (MV Agusta) leads eventual race winner Mike Hailwood (Honda) at de Strubben during the 1967 500cc Dutch TT. (Mick Woollett) Rear: Final fling – 39-year-old Hailwood on his way to victory in the 1979 500cc Senior TT on a works four-cylinder two-stroke Suzuki. This picture was taken at Whitegates, Ramsey. Mike set a lap record at 114.02mph (183.46kph) and won at the record speed of 111.75mph (179.81kph). (Bill Snelling, FoTTofinders)

Frontispiece
Learning curve – Mike Hailwood leads his new MV Agusta team-mate Giacomo Agostini during the 1965 East German Grand Prix at the Sachsenring. They finished first and second, and in his foreword Agostini says that he learned a lot from Mike that year. Note the kerbstones and the glistening wet circuit. (Wolfgang Gruber)

Contents

Introduction

Such is the fame and charisma of Mike Hailwood that 30 years after he won his ninth World Championship and 20 years since he finally quit racing after his incredible TT comeback rides, the readers of a Swiss motorsport magazine voted him the best motorcycle racer of all time. And that despite the fact that the only event he ever contested in Switzerland was a hill climb in which he crashed and broke a collarbone!

Yet strangely enough, despite his worldwide fame and his awesome record of successes in every class and on every size and type of racing motorcycle from 50cc two-stroke Itom to 864cc vee-twin four-stroke Ducati, no-one has previously attempted a book of this type about him. There have been two excellent biographies – the first by his friend and mentor Ted Macauley and a more recent one by motorsport specialist Chris Hilton – but until now no book has traced the story of his almost unbelievably hectic racing career in chronological order, backed by a comprehensive results section and lavishly illustrated.

Luck, as is so often the case in all our lives, played its part in the birth of this project. As road race reporter of *Motor Cycle News* I had reported Mike's very first meet-ing at Oulton Park in April 1957, and as editor of *Motor Cycle* his last TT in 1979. In the 23 seasons between those dates I believe I reported more of his races than any other journalist.

In my semi-retirement it dawned on me that no-one had yet produced a worthwhile, modern book about Mike – a useful book that would not only tell his racing story but would back it up with a results section detail-ing every single race in which he ever rode. A book you can pull off the shelf to settle an argument about what he rode, when, where, and what happened. Checking my photographic files I found I already had over 200 prints of Mike – what a pity to waste them!

Gradually the idea grew, but it only blossomed when, by sheer good fortune, I bumped into Darryl Reach, one of the Editorial Directors of Haynes Publishing, at the Motorcycle Show at the NEC, Birmingham. In casual conversation I mentioned that I had been thinking about a Hailwood book and outlined what I had in mind. Darryl could hardly believe it, because he had the same idea. In fact he had already put the wheels in motion and was looking for an author!

Within weeks the joint project was under way. My

first task was to make certain we had sufficient top-class photographs and here again luck was on my side, for both Nick Nicholls, who covered the British scene during the Hailwood era, and Austrian Wolfgang Gruber, who photographed the Continental Grands Prix, were not only alive and well but were ready, willing, and able to provide the necessary prints from their archives. Like me, and just about everyone else who ever met him, Nick and Wolfgang are Hailwood fans, and in response to my request for photographs the latter wrote: 'It is fantastic that a book will be published about the greatest rider on two wheels we have ever seen – and what a nice guy he always was!' Additional pictures were provided by Don Morley, Carlo Perelli, Roland Priess, and Bill Snelling. A special word of thanks must also go to Mike's sister Chris Buckler, who lent me early pictures from the family album to illustrate the opening chapter.

For the results, information, and quotes from articles I did with Mike I delved deeply into the file copies of the magazines I worked for at the time; first Cyril

The author and his wife Peta with Mike Hailwood at Brands Hatch in 1965. (Mick Woollett)

Quantrill's infant *Motor Cycle News*, then *Motor Cycling*, and finally *Motor Cycle*, which changed its title to *Motor Cycle Weekly* towards the end. When I approached the copyright owners for permission to use quotes from the publications in which I had chronicled Mike's doings on a week-to-week basis it was generously given: by Robin Miller, a former *MCN* reporter and Hailwood fan who is now chairman of the EMAP group; by his colleague Ian Templeton, the current publisher of *MCN*; and by

Wolfgang Gruber shows Mike his 1972 calendar at the September 1971 'Race of the Year' meeting at Mallory Park. (Wolfgang Gruber)

Malcolm Wheeler of Mortons Motorcycle Media, who recently bought the copyright to much of the pre-1971 *MCN*, *Motor Cycling* and *Motor Cycle* material. Thank you, gentlemen.

Thank you also to Giacomo Agostini, the world's most successful racing motorcyclist, with 15 World Championships and 122 Grands Prix wins (including ten TTs) to his credit, for his Foreword. He was one of less than a handful of riders to race against the maestro on equal terms and his tribute gives a genuine insight into Mike's character.

This book has involved a lot of hard work, first by slogging through the old weeklies to dig out the results,

B.R. 'Nick' Nicholls in 1960, during the early Hailwood era.
(B.R. Nicholls)

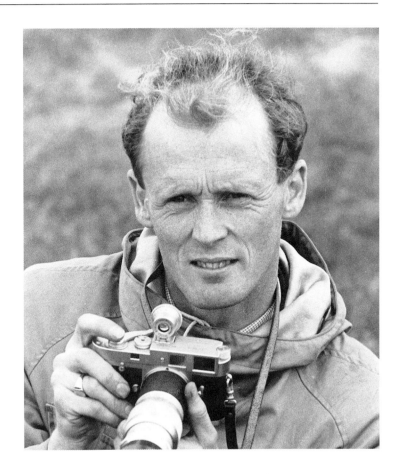

race by race, and sifting through millions of words to find those involving Mike; then writing the story; and finally sorting through over 600 black-and-white prints and nearly 100 colour transparencies to bring you what I consider to be the best. But it has been an immensely enjoyable task, and one made easier by the help of Darryl Reach and his colleague Alison Roelich, who coped admirably with my antiquated working methods, including a typewritten manuscript hammered out on the same Olympia portable that I used when reporting Mike's last TT!

I hope you will find it a worthwhile and fitting tribute to the man who rode 18 different makes of machine in at least 725 races and won 366 of them. He was, in my opinion, the greatest racing motorcyclist of all time, and as Wolfgang put it so succinctly, 'what a nice guy he always was!'

Mick Woollett
Flaunden, Hertfordshire
March 2000

Foreword

by Giacomo Agostini

Winner of 15 World Championships and 122 Grands Prix

Mike Hailwood – what memories his name brings back to me. What a man, what a rider, what a gentleman. Yes, he was a gentleman both on and off the track. He was always very fair when he was racing. He liked to win by using his strength and skill, not by scheming or pushing, and this is very important. You could trust him, knowing that whatever the speed you were racing at and no matter how close you were, he would behave like a gentleman. Mike was only happy when he won 'fair and square'. He liked to win through his own skill and, of course, the power and handling of his machine, and not because his rivals had problems.

I remember especially the Isle of Man TT in 1967, when we had such a fantastic race. It had always been my ambition to beat Mike in a TT race. To beat the best rider on his favourite circuit – that was a dream, an ambition, for me. Do you remember that race? We both broke the lap record, first me and then Mike. There was never more than seconds in it, but when I saw from my signals that I was leading Mike by a few seconds with just over a lap to go I could hardly believe it. To beat Mike in the Isle of Man was nearly impossible, but at that moment it seemed that I could do it. Then the chain of my MV Agusta broke! Imagine my disappointment. It was the end of my dream. I had been so close to winning, but after two hours of the hardest possible racing on the world's toughest circuit the chance was gone in a split second.

But the point of my story is that Mike was not happy with that win. I remember that when he went to the podium he never smiled. Unlike others who were happy when a rival broke down he only wanted to win through his own talent, his own skill. That was the gentleman on the track. I went to my hotel, and I don't mind admitting that I cried for an hour. That race had meant so much to me. Then Mike showed just what sort of a man he was off the track. Instead of celebrating the win with his friends he came round to my hotel, picked me up and took me out to dinner. After that we went dancing with the girls. That's what I mean by a gentleman off the track.

To me he was the best rider and I learned a lot from him. He was already a star when I was just beginning. I remember how in those early days I used to go to see him race in the Italian meetings whenever I could, to study his technique, to see what he did with the bike.

Then, after I had made my name racing for Morini, I was signed by Count Domenico Agusta for the 1965 season. Mike was the established star and many in his position would have been jealous of a younger rider joining him, especially an Italian who might be favoured by the management. But if he was jealous he never showed it.

I had a lot to learn that first year. Remember, I was moving up from a 250cc single-cylinder to the big old 350 and 500cc four-cylinder machines on which Mike already had three years' experience. So during practice I would try to follow him. Some riders might have objected to this and tried all sorts of tricks to stop the 'new boy' from following them. But not Mike. He just got on with what he was doing and luckily for me he always started slowly and built up his speed lap by lap, which was good for me. It gave me a chance to follow and learn from him. Yes, looking back I learnt everything from him. And then, of course, when he went to Honda in 1966 we became rivals.

For two years we fought for the 350 and 500cc World Championships – two fantastic seasons and many hard, hard races, but he always fought fair. He rode very hard on the track but we remained friends. Mike never took the racing so very seriously – he enjoyed a laugh, a joke, a party, too much for that.

I've told you that my toughest race and my most disappointing was the 1967 Senior TT. I think my best race against Mike was the 500cc 1967 Belgian Grand Prix at the very fast Francorchamps circuit. The Honda was faster but my MV Agusta handled better. It was a long race, over 200km (125 miles), so we both had to start with full tanks. I knew that I would have the advantage when the bikes were so heavy, so I decided to try very hard for the first two laps and see what happened. Well, my tactics worked – by then I had a good lead, and this time my bike gave no trouble and I won. Of course, I know the big Honda was very hard to ride and the gearbox was a problem. Mike finished second that day and congratulated me. I think in a way he was happy for me because the Belgian was only just over two weeks after the TT.

Then to make that winning comeback at the TT 11 years later – fantastic! But of course, he knew the Isle of

Two of the greatest TT riders of all time – Giacomo Agostini (left) and Mike Hailwood relax before the start of their epic 1967 Senior TT battle, which ended with a win for Hailwood. (Mick Woollett)

Man and he loved racing there. That was why it was possible at 38 years old and with a leg badly damaged in a car crash. It nevertheless took a special kind of man to do that. But then Mike was a very special man.

CHAPTER 1

Carefully laid plans

On the morning of Easter Monday, 22 April 1957, two men whose paths were to cross repeatedly over the next 23 years made their separate ways to the Oulton Park circuit in the Cheshire countryside. First to arrive, as a passenger in his millionaire father's magnificent white Bentley Continental, was a slim, shy unknown by the name of Mike Hailwood. He had celebrated his 17th birthday earlier the same month and was due to make his racing début that day on a scarlet 125cc MV Agusta. Later, when practising was already under way, the second rode into the paddock on a 500cc BSA Gold Star with Watsonian Monaco sidecar. This was the author, who had ridden to Oulton to report the meeting for the infant *Motor Cycle News*, founded by Cyril Quantrill just over a year previously and struggling to survive against the might of the long-established *Motor Cycle* and *Motor Cycling*.

Those were very different times. Petrol was still

The first race Mike rode in was at Oulton Park, Cheshire, on 22 April 1957 – and here he poses on his 125cc MV Agusta just before the race, in which he finished 11th. (Courtesy of Christine Buckler)

strictly rationed following the Suez crisis (a gallon a week for most motorcyclists), a quarter of all motorcycles on British roads were fitted with a sidecar, there was not a single mile of motorway open, and Bill Haley and his Comets had just arrived in England to spread the new craze for rock-and-roll music. Young Hailwood made no impression that day. Under the watchful eyes of his father Stan and veteran racer Bill Webster, who had lent him the little MV Agusta, he finished 11th and merited no mention in my race report. The winner was the former World Champion Cecil Sandford, riding a Mondial, while the stars in the bigger classes were John Surtees (MV Agusta), Terry Shepherd (Norton), and John Hartle (Norton).

Five days later we were both at Castle Combe, and there Mike improved significantly. In my report of the 125cc race for *MCN*, I wrote: 'The two streamlined MVs of Mike O'Rourke and Dudley Edlin were followed home by the naked models of Rees and Hailwood who provided the excitement by dicing for third place throughout the race.' Rees took the place. The references to 'streamlined' and 'naked' machines were made because at that time the regulations allowed the 'full bin' style of fairing which enclosed the front wheel, banned at the end of the 1957 season. Later that day Mike made his début in the 250cc class and finished fifth on a 175cc MV Agusta. Two weeks later Mike scored his first rostrum placing when he finished third in the 200cc class at Brands Hatch on the 175cc MV Agusta, beaten by O'Rourke and Edlin but ahead of Dave Chadwick (MV Agusta), who was already an established star.

The carefully laid plans of his father Stan were beginning to bear fruit. A competitor himself in the interwar years, first on sidecars (a gammy leg ruled out solos) and later in cars at Brooklands, he had made his money from the 'Kings of Oxford' chain of motorcycle shops. Now he was determined to see his only son succeed. But Stan, always tanned from holidays in the south of France and the Caribbean, was a hard man and a realist. He knew that if Mike did not have the natural talent nothing in the world could make him a star in the rough and tumble world of motorcycle road racing. First he made sure that Mike had the best possible bikes – and in the early days that meant 125 and 175cc single cylinder, four-stroke MV Agustas. Then he employed a full-time mechanic to look after them and equipped him with a van to transport the bikes from meeting to meeting. Finally he targeted the media and made sure that the 'gentlemen of the press' sat up and took notice of what young Mike was up to.

I can well remember Stan's unmistakable figure limping towards me at a meeting – his smiling, bronzed, Clark Gable features with silver pencil-moustache, topped by a wide-brimmed brown trilby and clothed in a trade-mark long, belted cream raincoat. But while his mouth smiled, his piercing blue eyes did not. He was not a man for idle talk or chit-chat. On this occasion he came straight to the point: 'Keep an eye on young Mike and give us a good write-up … and remember I'm one of your paper's biggest advertisers.' The message was clear, and it would have been easy to dislike the whole Hailwood set-up, and Mike in particular. But he was so completely different to his father, so modest and unassuming, that you could not help but like him. And fortunately for me his talent was such that I was forced to write well of him anyway, by the sheer quality of his performances.

Born on 2 April 1940 and christened Stanley Michael Bailey Hailwood, he first started riding when he was seven, around the grounds of the family home in Oxfordshire where he lived with his elder sister Chris, his step-mother Pat, and his father Stan. The first bike he rode was a one-off miniature machine powered by a 100cc Royal Enfield two-stroke engine, but Mike could only ride it during the holidays because even at that tender age he was away at a boarding preparatory school. From there he went to Pangbourne Nautical College, an expensive public school near Reading. This establishment prided itself on tradition and nautical discipline and was not to Mike's liking. His twin ambitions at the time were to become a naval officer and to race motorcycles. However, his naval aspirations gradually waned as he became increasingly bored by the subject's academic demands, and he eventually persuaded his father to let him leave at the age of 16, before he had finished the course. Mike later recalled that the only things he really enjoyed at Pangbourne – apart from wearing the smart naval uniform – were boxing and music. His success in the ring (he had 14 fights for the school, winning 13 and drawing the other one) pleased his father, who had also been a keen boxer in his youth, and helped soften the blow of Mike's early departure from the college.

After a few months working in the Oxford branch of Stan's motorcycle business his father got him a job at the Triumph factory in Meriden. The idea was for young Mike to learn the trade, starting with where the bikes came from. He began as tea-boy and progressed to the assembly line – and was bored to tears.

Despite his burning ambition to race, Mike did not ride a fast, sporting bike on the roads. He commuted from his lodgings near the Triumph factory in Meriden on a very humdrum old 250cc AJS with a top speed of perhaps 60mph (96.5kph), content to jog along rather than play racers. Neither did he go to many meetings as a spectator – he wanted to race for himself, not watch others, and he could not wait for 2 April 1957, when he would be 17 and able to get a racing licence.

There is no doubt that father Stan was the driving force in those early days. Used to controlling a large staff and a business empire with a branch in just about every major British town, he brought organisation and discipline to the family racing effort. Bike and rider had to be immaculately turned out and there was a thorough post-mortem after every event, to pin-point where improvements could be made.

After the steady improvement shown during the first three meetings Mike was absent from the tracks for a month, because, even before he had started racing, his father had already entered him for the tough Scottish Six Days Trial and had persuaded Triumph to lend him a 200cc Sports Cub. Henry Vale, boss of Triumph's experimental department, remembers the episode: 'It was ridiculous really. It was a perfectly standard bike, not prepared for the trial, and as far as I know Mike had never ridden in an event of this type. He hated the whole idea, thought it was a waste of time and retired early to get back to road racing.'

His next race was on the tricky circuit which used roads around an army camp at Blandford. In those days it was a major event that attracted crowds of 40,000 – and it was there, on Whit Monday, 10 June 1957, that Mike scored his first win, on his MV Agusta, in the 125cc race. In the space of exactly seven weeks and just four meetings he had progressed from novice to winner! His natural talent, that instinctive skill which allowed him to get the absolute best out of every machine he raced, was beginning to shine through. But there were still lessons to be learned, and just four days after his Blandford triumph he came a cropper while racing his 175cc MV Agusta at Scarborough. He collided with another rider, crashed, and dislocated a thumb as well as suffering a gashed arm and knee.

The doctor suggested a six-week lay-off, but Mike was back in a month, riding at the British Motor Cycle Racing Club's Trophy Day meeting at Silverstone. He finished second in both 250cc races there, riding his bigger MV Agusta with its capacity now enlarged from 175 to 203cc. Just a week later the MV Agusta carried him to his first 250cc win, at Snetterton, where he also finished third in the 125cc class.

The next milestone was his first double win, which was achieved on Saturday 27 July on his first visit to the tortuous little half-mile (0.8km) circuit at Rhydymwyn in North Wales. There Mike won the 125 and 250cc

classes on his MV Agustas, successes that earned him a special mention in Cyril Quantrill's 'Gossip' column in *MCN*. But once again success was followed by failure. A week after his first 'double', Mike – out for the first time with a 'full bin' streamlining on his 203cc MV Agusta – crashed heavily at Oulton Park and broke a collarbone. Earlier in the day he had finished second on an Itom in his début in the 50cc class and third in the 125cc race, and I wrote in my report for *MCN*: 'The meeting was marred by a number of accidents ... and up-and-coming young lightweight rider Mike Hailwood ... fell in the 200cc championship breaking a collarbone.'

This injury threw a spanner into Stan's carefully laid plans, for Mike had already gained enough points from his race successes to qualify for an international racing licence and was entered for his first classic event – the Ulster Grand Prix, which was then a round of the World Championship series. That was to be held the very next weekend, so competing was obviously out of the question for Mike. In fact he did not return to the track until 8 September, when he raced at Brands Hatch. There he won the 200cc race on his bigger MV Agusta, with its capacity reduced to 196cc, and achieved another benchmark by breaking his first record, the race record for the class. Later in the day he finished second on the same bike in the 250cc race, beaten by Dick Harding on his Velocette special.

The next weekend he went north to compete in his first international meeting, the Scarborough Gold Cup, which was, in those days, one of the major events of the British season. This was the same narrow and dangerous track where he had suffered his first racing crash back in June, but, undeterred, he battled it out with the stars to finish third in the 250cc class, beaten only by Dave Chadwick (MV Agusta) and the German Horst Kassner (NSU). Racing there myself (like Mike I finished third, but as sidecar passenger with Swiss rider Edgar Strub on his BMW) as well as reporting for *MCN*, I wrote of Scarborough: 'John Surtees was so impressed by the way Mike Hailwood rode his standard MV into third place that he is to lend Mike his own 250cc Sportmax NSU for the Hutchinson 100 at Silverstone this Saturday.' However, his third crash of the season, while practising at Silverstone, ruled him out of both the meeting and the rest of the British season with a broken ankle. The path to the top was proving a painful one.

All went quiet until mid-November. By that time I had taken over writing the weekly gossip column in *MCN* from editor Cyril Quantrill, and we had renamed it 'Paddock Gossip'. In the 13 November issue I wrote: 'A reader wrote in last week enquiring about Mike Hailwood's plans following the advertisement offering Mike's MVs for sale that appeared last week. The answer is Mike certainly is not giving up. In fact he sails for a season's racing in South Africa on November 21. He is taking a 350cc Norton and a 250cc NSU with him and will compete in all the events he can get to.'

Both bikes were new to him. Stan had bought the NSU from John Surtees and had acquired a nearly-new 350cc Manx Norton. The whole trip to South Africa had been carefully planned by Stan to further Mike's racing education. The experienced Dave Chadwick, who had raced in South Africa the previous season, was to travel and race with him and they were accompanied by Mike's full-time mechanic John Dadley. They were to race under Stan's 'Ecurie Sportive' banner, which included the slogan 'For Love of the Sport' on van and bikes and the motto 'Nil Desperandum'. All of this attracted a certain amount of ribald comment from their often hard-up rivals, which Mike enjoyed as much as anyone, while thick-skinned Stan – not known for his sense of humour – remained oblivious.

Their first race in South Africa was at the Roy Hesketh circuit at Pietermaritzburg, near Durban. Mike made an immediate impression on fellow competitors there, including future world champions Gary Hocking and Jim Redman, by winning the 250cc race first time out on the NSU. Stan flew out for his son's second meeting – the Port Elizabeth 200, on New Year's Day 1958. This was a handicap event, open to all sizes of machine and run on a genuine near ten-mile (16km) road circuit south of the city. Despite his youth – he was still only 17 – Mike was last man away of the 250s. He stormed through the field with a record lap for the class at 90.76mph (146.03kph), but could not catch the early starters – the handicapping had been just too severe. Team-mate Chadwick (Norton) won the 350cc division,

with Redman (Norton) top in the 500cc class. They then returned to Pietermaritzburg, where Mike faced real opposition in the form of local hero Borro Castellani mounted on an ex-works Mondial. This was a tough one, because the fiery South African – famous for his lurid riding style – was determined to beat this young upstart. With a record lap at 71.45mph (114.96kph) Mike was nevertheless the winner, but he had to race the NSU so hard that it seized in the later handicap race.

Further 250cc wins followed at a third Pietermaritzburg meeting and at the Grand Central circuit between Johannesburg and Pretoria. It was there that Mike finally made his début on the 350cc Norton – his first race on anything bigger than a 250 and his first on a Norton. Why he had waited so long to race the Manx is not clear. Some say that he was afraid to move up into the bigger class where the opposition was very much tougher. Whatever the reason, the race ended in disappointment, for he retired with a broken con-rod. The Norton failed again at a meeting at St Albans aerodrome near Port Elizabeth, where Chadwick won both 350 and 500cc races and where there was no 250cc class. The South African venture ended at the Easter River circuit near Cape Town, at which Mike won the 250cc class with a record lap and finished second to Chadwick (350cc Norton) in the overall handicap. Mechanic Dadley then took the NSU engine out of the frame, and Mike flew back to London with the unit as excess baggage – which cost the then-astronomical sum of £100.

He arrived on 1 April, the day before his 18th birthday, accompanied not only by the NSU engine but by an impressive array of cups and trophies, and as the reigning South African 250cc National Champion – his first title. Stan had been busy in the meantime. He had bought a second NSU Sportmax from an advertisement he spotted in *MCN* and had set up interviews for Mike on both BBC radio and television, in which he was dubbed 'the fastest teenager on earth'. The Hailwood bandwagon was well and truly rolling.

Four days after arriving home Mike was in action at Brands Hatch. He won the 200cc race on his bigger MV Agusta and finished second on an NSU to local maestro

Derek Minter riding Bob Geeson's very fast REG twin. Three days later, on Easter Monday, he won both classes at Crystal Palace. These successes inspired another mention in *MCN*'s 'Paddock Gossip': 'There is no doubt about it. Young Mike Hailwood has racing in his blood. He is the son of Stan Hailwood, director of Kings of Oxford and himself a popular racing motorist of the 1920s.'

The next weekend he was at Mallory Park, making a double début – his first UK outing in the 350cc class and his first anywhere on a 500cc bike. Both were Nortons, the bigger machine purchased from John Surtees. In a top-class field he came through from a poor start to finish fifth in the smaller category, but was unplaced in the larger. He won the 125cc race at the International 'Silverstone Saturday' meeting six days later but dropped out of the 250cc with engine trouble. Another week later he contested all four classes at Castle Combe, where he won the two lightweight events – beating Minter and the REG in the 250cc – and finished sixth in both big bike races. No-one had ever seriously attempted all four classes before, yet here was a skinny just-18-year-old not only doing it but winning as well! The following weekend yet another milestone was reached when Mike won the 350cc race at Brands Hatch in style, beating 'King of Brands' Minter fair and square, both men riding similar Manx Nortons. He also won the 200cc and 250cc events – the first time he had won three classes in a day. Only in the 500cc race did he fail, crashing while in sixth place.

The Hailwood bandwagon then rolled up to Aintree en route to two Irish events. On the circuit inside the world-famous Grand National horse-racing course he contested only the lightweight classes and was beaten into second place in both by local star Fron Purslow. In Ireland he won the 200cc handicap event but retired from the 250cc at Cookstown before being involved, a few days later, in one of the closest finishes ever seen at the North West 200, when Sammy Miller beat him by a second to win the 250cc class, in which both rode NSUs.

Despite the fact that he was due to make his TT début and had entered all four solo classes, Mike then dashed back to Brands Hatch for the Whit Monday (26 May)

meeting instead of crossing to the Isle of Man early to learn the two very different circuits the races were then run on – the traditional 37.7-mile (60.66km) mountain lap still in use today and the 10-mile (16.1km) Clypse course introduced for the sidecar and lightweight classes in 1954. At Brands he missed the 200cc class but won the 250 and 350cc and scored his first placing in the 500cc when he finished second to Bob Anderson (Norton). Just a week later he finished 12th on a Norton in his first TT, the Junior for 350cc bikes (the race name referring to engine size rather than to the capability or age of the riders).

Two days later, on the Wednesday, Mike was out on the Clypse circuit for the two lightweight races. For the first race, the 125cc, he had a new mount, a double overhead camshaft, single-cylinder Paton built by former Mondial mechanic Giuseppe Pattoni and acquired by Ecurie Sportive following negotiations which involved both myself and my Italian opposite number Carlo Perelli, sports editor of *Motociclismo*. Mike finished seventh on this bike, but was more successful in the afternoon on his NSU, which was now tuned by former Brooklands star Bill Lacey, finishing third, being beaten only by the works MV Agustas ridden by Tarquinio Provini and Carlo Ubbiali.

Mike's first TT week finished with a sensible ride into 13th place on his Norton in the 500cc Senior race at an average of 92.24mph (148.41kph). At this time Stan Hailwood was using two tuners to prepare Mike's engines. Originally Francis Beart had been favoured and it was he who built Mike's first 350cc Norton; he also sold Stan a special 500cc Norton unit. But gradually Bill Lacey came more and more into the picture. A motorcycle World Record holder in the early 1930s (including the important one-hour record which he captured on his home-tuned 500cc Norton at 110.80mph/178.28kph in 1931), Lacey had moved on to preparing racing cars. Stan had kept in touch with him since his old Brooklands days and persuaded him to take over the preparation of Mike's bikes – first the Paton and NSU and then the Nortons – working in his Slough premises only 20 miles (32km) from the Hailwood home at Highmoor Hall, Nettlebed.

From the TT, Ecurie Sportive went straight to Mallory

Park, where Mike won the 250 and 350cc races but retired from the big-bike race with engine trouble. Six days later he was racing in the lightweight classes at Scarborough, retiring from the 150cc race when the carburettor stub of the Paton broke but winning the 250cc on his NSU. An overnight dash took the entourage the 200 miles (322km) to Snetterton and there Mike enjoyed his most successful day's racing to date – three wins, followed by a second place to arch-rival Minter (Norton) in the 500cc event, plus new lap records in all four classes! Then came a complete change of machines – from four out-and-out racers to a 650cc Triumph Tiger 110 for the Thruxton 500-mile (804.5km) Sports Bike endurance event. There Mike shared the riding of the factory-prepared bike with Dan Shorey from Banbury, and the two of them ran away with the race.

Within days Mike was in Holland to compete in his first Continental event, the Dutch TT which was, and still is, Holland's biggest one-day sporting event, annually attracting crowds of over 150,000 to the circuit near Assen. By this time Ecurie Sportive had acquired a third 125cc machine – a Ducati – to supplement the Paton and the MV Agusta. In Holland Mike decided to race the Ducati in the smallest class but could only finish tenth. He fared better in the 250cc, taking fourth spot on his NSU, and finished his day's racing with a fifth place in the 350cc class riding the Norton, in a race dominated by the works MV Agustas of Surtees and John Hartle. He was unable to ride in the 500cc class because the sport's governing body, the Fédération Internationale Motocycliste (FIM), imposed a limit of 500 racing kilometres (310 miles) a day, and to have ridden in four classes would have exceeded this.

Instead of going on to the Belgian Grand Prix the following weekend as most top-liners did, Mike returned to race in the British Motor Cycle Racing Club's low-profile Trophy Day meeting at Silverstone. There he equalled his Snetterton score with three wins and a second in the 500cc class, in which he was beaten by Geoff Duke protégé Alan Rutherford (Norton). An oiled plug at the start of the 500cc race foiled Mike's attempt to win all four classes at Castle Combe the next Saturday, 12 July. However, he did win four races – the 125, 250 and 350cc, and an overall handicap event in which he rode the NSU.

Then it was off to the Continent again – first for the German Grand Prix, held on the 14-mile (22.5km) Nürburgring, and then up to Hedemora for the Swedish Grand Prix. In Germany the NSU front brake locked so viciously that the axle was bent, forcing retirement, but Mike went well on his Norton in the 350cc race to finish fourth ahead of a host of star names including Bob Anderson, Dickie Dale, Gary Hocking, Luigi Taveri and Jack Ahearn. Just a week later he claimed his first-ever Continental World Championship rostrum positions by twice finishing among the first three in the Swedish Grand Prix. His first came in the 350cc race, in which he finished third behind the legendary Geoff Duke (Norton) and Bob Anderson (Norton). Then, in the later 250cc event, he took advantage of the mechanical failure of both the works MV Agustas to finish second on his NSU, beaten only by the super-fast factory MZ two-stroke twin of Horst Fugner. It was Mike's best placing in a World Championship race so far and it proved beyond a shadow of doubt that the shy 18-year-old had well and truly arrived.

The Hailwoods enjoying a skiing holiday in St Moritz, Switzerland, in early 1951. With Mike and father Stan is Mike's sister Christine. (Courtesy of Christine Buckler)

Left *Another picture from that first Oulton Park meeting shows Mike astride his 125cc MV Agusta getting some hints and tips from Bert North, who managed his father's Manchester 'Kings of Oxford' motorcycle shop.* (Courtesy of Christine Buckler)

Below *For Mike's second meeting, at Castle Combe on 27 April 1957, the 125cc MV Agusta had been joined by a 175cc model for the 250cc class. Here Mike and Stan ready the bikes on which Mike finished fourth and fifth.* (Courtesy of Christine Buckler)

Right *A delighted Mike wheels in his MV Agusta after finishing fourth in a hard-fought 125cc race at Castle Combe in April 1957.* (Courtesy of Christine Buckler)

Below right *The winning team! Ten-year-old Mike rides pillion with his father Stan on a 500cc side-valve BSA at Ferry House, Goring, shortly before they moved to Highmoor Hall in Nettlebed, Oxfordshire.* (Courtesy of Christine Buckler)

Left *Fifteen-year-old Mike in the uniform he wore as a student at the Pangbourne Nautical College.* (Courtesy of Christine Buckler)

Below *One subject that Mike excelled in whilst at Pangbourne was music. Here he poses (at the back) with the College band at an end-of-term concert.* (Courtesy of Christine Buckler)

Right *Determined style at Scarborough in June 1957 as Mike hurls his 175cc MV Agusta into a bend – but minutes later he crashed and dislocated a thumb, an injury which put him out of action for three weeks.* (Don Morley)

Left *Full streamlining, banned at the end of the year, was still allowed in 1957, when Mike used it on his bigger MV Agusta at Oulton Park in August – with disastrous results! He crashed and broke a collarbone. Here he's seen in action during the race.* (B.R. Nicholls)

Right *Seventeen-year-old Mike smiles for the camera at Silverstone in September 1957, where a crash while practising ruled him out of the meeting with a broken ankle.* (B.R. Nicholls)

Below *Sunny days in South Africa. Mike (left, astride his NSU) with friends at the Port Elizabeth 200 on New Year's Day 1958, where he won the 250cc class. Dave Chadwick, who toured with him, sits on his Norton with mechanic John Dadley crouching between them.* (Courtesy of Christine Buckler)

Left *Mike with the ex-John Surtees NSU Sportmax that carried him to a string of wins during his 1957–8 season in South Africa. This picture was taken at the Port Elizabeth 200.* (Courtesy of Christine Buckler)

Below *Hand on the rev counter of his 250cc NSU Sportmax, Mike admires Steve Podmore's 175cc MV Agusta, while mechanic John Dadley and Dave Chadwick (left) look on.* (Courtesy of Christine Buckler)

Right *Competitors old and young. Frank Cope (centre), a 61-year-old Birmingham motorcycle dealer, with 17-year-old Mike Hailwood (right) and Dave Chadwick in South Africa early in 1958.* (Courtesy of Christine Buckler)

Below right *Brands Hatch on Good Friday, 4 April 1958, and Mike heads for a win in the 200cc race on the larger of his two MV Agustas.* (B.R. Nicholls)

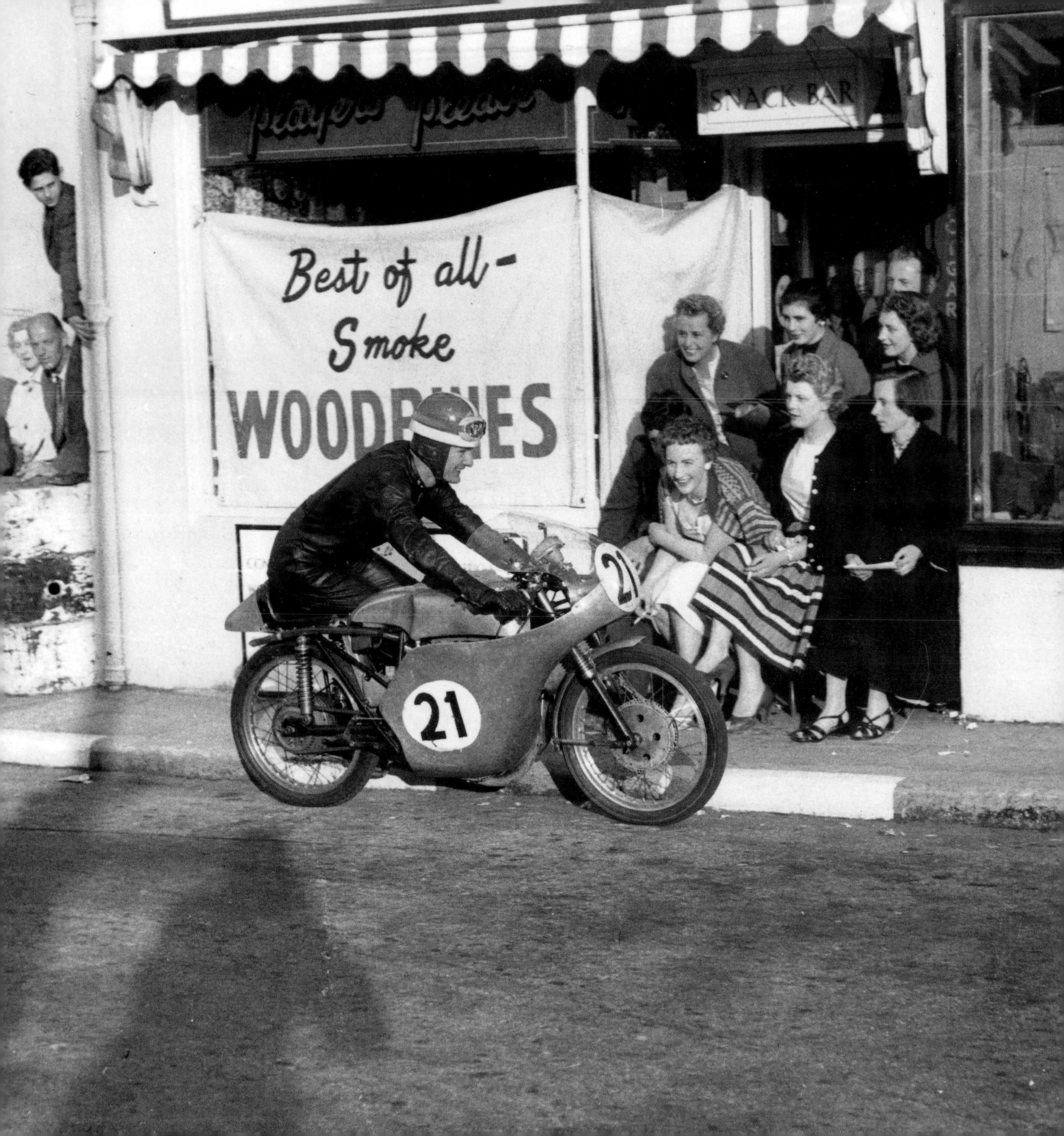
SNACK BAR
Best of all-
Smoke
21
21

Left *A broken valve stopped Mike's 125cc Paton in Onchan village during practice for the 1958 TT. Here he exchanges banter with spectators in a shop doorway.* (B.R. Nicholls)

Right *First practice session on the TT Mountain circuit late May 1958, and Mike speeds through Union Mills on his 350cc Norton. A dolphin fairing was fitted later in the week.* (B.R. Nicholls)

Below *Mike's first TT was the 1958 Junior. Here he rounds Ramsey Hairpin on his 350cc Norton on his way to 12th place.* (B.R. Nicholls)

Left *After competing on the Mountain circuit, Mike's second TT in 1958 was the 125cc Lightweight on the shorter Clypse course. Here he heads for seventh place on his Paton. (B.R. Nicholls)*

Below *Flat out on the ex-Surtees Sportmax NSU in the 1958 250cc Lightweight TT, in which he finished a magnificent third, beaten only by the works MV Agustas. (B.R. Nicholls)*

Right *Spectators get a birds-eye view as Mike rounds Governors Bridge on his NSU on his way to a fine third place in the 1958 250cc Lightweight TT. (B.R. Nicholls)*

Far right *Last race of the 1958 TT week. Mike leaps his 500cc Norton over Ballaugh Bridge on his way to 13th place. At 18 he was the youngest competitor and the only one to finish all four solo races. (B.R. Nicholls)*

Below right *In late June 1958 Mike and co-rider Dan Shorey won the Thruxton 500 Mile Race for catalogue sports machines, riding a 650cc Triumph. Here Mike is presented with a painting of himself in action in the event by Triumph boss Edward Turner, while father Stan looks on. (Mick Woollett)*

"THRUXTON 500 MILE" WINNER

CHAPTER 2

A blur
of activity

The 1958 season ended in a blur of activity for the Hailwood equipe. In the space of just ten weeks Mike rode at 13 different meetings, from Zandvoort in Holland in the east to the Ulster Grand Prix in the west, and from Scarborough in the north to the end-of-season gathering at Brands Hatch in the south. In all he rode in 38 races ranging from 125cc to 500cc, won 22 of them, was placed in the first three in a further six, and crashed twice. During this spell he raced seven different makes of machine and won all the major solo classes at two events (Mallory Park and Snetterton). No wonder he won three of the four ACU Road Racing Stars, awarded to the rider who scored most points in selected national meetings by the Auto Cycle Union, who govern the sport in Great Britain. Mike took the honours in the 125, 250 and 350cc classes and finished fifth in the 500cc division, which was won by his friend and fellow

The two men who won all four ACU Road Racing Stars in 1958 battle it out at Cadwell Park in September that year, with 500cc champion Tony Godfrey leading from Mike, who won the 125, 250 and 350cc awards. Here both are riding 500cc Nortons. (Mick Woollett)

jazz lover Tony Godfrey. He was next voted second to double World Champion John Surtees in the *MCN* Man of the Year contest, decided by the readers' votes, and won the annual Pinhard Prize as the outstanding under-21 motorcyclist of the year ahead of moto-cross star Dave Bickers.

Curiously, amid all this success, Mike had to deny a persistent rumour that he intended to retire at the end of the year, though he did admit to having no definite plans. That the equipe was going to continue was confirmed when Stan negotiated the purchase of 125 and 250cc ex-works Mondials from Epsom dealer-racer Arthur Wheeler. In fact Mike made a winning début on the smaller Mondial at the penultimate meeting of the British season at the Crystal Palace circuit, and followed this up by winning first time out on the 250cc model at Brands Hatch the next weekend (12 October). The available machinery was further strengthened when Stan bought three Manx Nortons from the Slazenger team, sponsored by the sports goods firm and actively supported by the Norton factory, which by that time had no team of its own.

To continue his racing education, and to keep in trim

for the next season in Europe, it was decided that Mike would do another season in South Africa. By this time the team had two mechanics and it was Jim Adams who travelled out by sea, taking with him two Nortons and the faithful old NSU Sportmax. I wrote in *MCN* at the time: 'With several Show week commitments Mike has to delay his departure until Friday week. He will fly out and is hoping that the machines will arrive safely on November 27 in time to re-jet and tune them for the new climatic conditions before he races at Cape Town on the 29th.'

The show referred to was the annual Earls Court Motorcycle Show, and one of the 'commitments' was for Mike to receive from Edward Turner, the autocratic boss of Triumph, a watercolour painting of himself on the Triumph Tiger 110 during his winning ride at the Thruxton 500-Mile Race. Prominent in the picture sent out by the Triumph Press Office was Stan, who had probably organised the whole thing. There was no mention of the part played by co-rider Dan Shorey! Mike also received the Pinhard Prize during the Show – presented to him by former racer and editor of *Motor Cycling* Graham Walker (father of Formula 1 commentator Murray) – as well as the three ACU Stars and his award for finishing second in the *MCN* Man of the Year contest. Then, before he flew out to South Africa, Mike, Stan and tuner Bill Lacey attended the British Motor Cycle Racing Club's annual dinner to receive yet more trophies.

Finally, just before he left for the airport, Mike confirmed his plans for 1959 and I duly reported in *MCN* that 'Mike intends to compete in all four solo classes again next year and all his machines will be prepared by Bill Lacey.' However, the 350cc Norton that Mike raced in South Africa had been built by rival tuner Francis Beart, and in December I reported that Beart was building him a special lightweight 350cc Norton for the 1959 season.

The carefully laid plans for the season's first South African outing, at the Killarney circuit near Cape Town, bore fruit. Despite crashing during 250cc practising Mike won all three classes, equalling the 350cc lap record and beating the 250cc and 500cc records. His achievement on the bigger bike was all the more praiseworthy because the old record had been set by none

other than Geoff Duke, on a works four-cylinder Gilera.

There was unscheduled excitement on the long drive up from Cape Town to the second meeting at Pietermaritzburg – a tyre burst on their hired van and it turned completely over, landing back on its wheels but with the roof stove in. Fortunately neither Mike nor mechanic Jim Adams was seriously injured; nor were the three bikes badly damaged. Once they had arrived at the Roy Hesketh circuit, Mike went one better than he had in Cape Town by winning all three classes and establishing three new lap records, despite competing against all the local hot-shots including Jim Redman, Paddy Driver, and Stan Setaro. The diffident youngster who had hesitated to race a 350cc Norton the previous year had certainly grown up!

From Natal the team travelled south to Port Elizabeth for the traditional 200 race, on New Year's Day 1959. Mike elected to ride his 500cc Norton in this long-distance handicap event, and all went well during practice on the demanding, narrow, bumpy road circuit, on which wandering tortoises were a constant menace. In fact Mike bettered the official record by lapping at 107.5mph (172.97kph).

However, at the start of the race itself mechanic Jim Adams forgot to remove the rag that had been stuffed into the carburettor to keep dust out, and as Mike bumped the Norton into life this was sucked into the engine, bending the valves. He spluttered round for three laps before pulling in to watch 62-year-old Frank Cope, a motorcycle dealer from Birmingham, take advantage of a generous handicap to win the race on a special 250cc Manx Norton that the factory had built for him. Dave Chadwick, who had been Mike's companion in South Africa the previous year and had also joined the present tour, finished third, and at the next meeting, back at Pietermaritzburg, won both the big-bike races on his Nortons. Mike himself had a poor day here, being beaten by local star Jannie Stander on his incredible home-brewed Velocette in the 250cc class, and by Chadwick in the 350cc race when the rebuilt 500cc refused to fire at the start.

Meanwhile, while Mike raced and enjoyed himself in the South African sunshine, Stan was scheming to get even better machinery for the coming season. He went out to Italy, accompanied by racer-dealer Bill Webster (who spoke the language and knew the ropes), and arranged a deal whereby he would set up a company to import Ducati roadster machines in return for the loan of a works desmodromic Ducati for the 125cc class. The fact that Mike, still only 18, was to get a fully fledged factory bike for 1959 was big news, and was reported on the front page of *MCN* on 28 January under the headline 'Desmodromic Ducati for Hailwood'. Stan also visited Morini in search of a factory 250cc racer and said that he hoped to persuade them to lend Mike a works bike for some events, while there were rumours that Ducati were planning twin-cylinder 125 and 250cc machines. Not wasting any time, Stan opened Ducati Concessionaires Ltd in Manchester in early February and offered 100, 125, 175 and 203cc single-cylinder sports roadsters for sale.

The first news that Honda were planning to compete in the TT came that same month, and *MCN* carried a road-test, by Dutch correspondent Gerhard Klomps, of 'the first Japanese motorcycle to reach Europe – the 250cc overhead camshaft Honda Dream'. Klomps prefaced his test report by saying: 'Up to now, we in Europe have heard little about the new Japanese motorcycle and scooter industry that has grown up since the war, but the Honda company is now a very large concern and last year produced 16,000 two-wheeled vehicles.' Little did we know then that within two decades Honda would become the world's largest motorcycle manufacturer, producing 11,000 bikes a day by 1980, or that the Japanese industry would annihilate the British factories.

With the South African season over, most of the top riders involved made their leisurely way back to Europe aboard the Union Castle liner *Edinburgh Castle*. Amongst those on board for the two-week trip were Mike, Dave Chadwick, Jim Redman, Paddy Driver, and mechanic Jim Adams, plus their assorted racing bikes. They arrived at Southampton on Friday 6 March, suntanned, relaxed, and raring to go. Mike confirmed that he was to be an official Ducati works rider in the 125cc class of the classics, teaming with Italians Alberto Gandossi and Bruno Spaggiari. He was to be supplied with two new desmodromic machines for the major

events, while the factory would rebuild his 1958 bike for British meetings. Additionally the factory were developing a 175cc twin for Italian events and would send one over for Mike to test to see if he felt an enlarged version had potential for the 250cc class.

First race of the 1959 UK season was at Mallory Park on Sunday 22 March, and it is worth noting that in those days running a sporting event on a Sunday was not without its problems. The powerful Lord's Day Observance Society would occasionally sue organisers who they felt were breaking the Sunday Observance Law of 1625, which declared it illegal to participate in or watch sport on a Sunday. This Society was a serious threat to all forms of motorcycle sport, because the majority of events were run on Sundays – so serious, in fact, that Geoff Duke and John Surtees headed a campaign to change the law, organised by the Sunday Freedom Association. Fortunately the courts hesitated to enforce the full rigours of the 1625 statute. It was agreed instead that Sunday events could be held, but that spectators must not pay to get in. The organisers got round this by letting people in free but then charging them for access to special viewing enclosures. How different from today, and another illustration of how our lives have changed in recent years.

Mallory was wet and miserable on race-day, and Mike retired from the 250cc event with water in the ignition system of his Mondial. He won the 350cc event but could do no better than fifth in the 500cc, won by Bob McIntyre. Mallory was followed by nine meetings on British circuits in the space of just seven weeks. First there were three over the Easter Weekend – Brands Hatch on Good Friday, Snetterton on Easter Sunday, and then Thruxton on the Monday. In all Mike rode in 13 races (plus two heats at Snetterton) and won eight of them (plus the two heats), and at Snetterton he made a little bit of motorcycle racing history when he won the 125cc event on a desmodromic Ducati – the first time a race on a British track had been won by a motorcycle equipped with this type of valve gear (in which the valves are closed as well as opened by mechanical means rather than valve springs).

At Thruxton he again won all four main solo classes racing the Ducati, the Mondial, and a brace of Nortons, but the next week he crashed at over 100mph (161kph) when testing at Silverstone and suffered heavy bruising. His next meeting was at the same circuit – the international 'Silverstone Saturday' event sponsored by *Motor Cycling* magazine – and Mike's condition was not eased by miserably cold, wet weather. He won the two lightweight classes despite these problems, but could only muster a fifth and a fourth in the 350 and 500cc divisions. At Mallory the next day he had what was becoming a more and more unusual experience – he did not win a single race! His 250cc Mondial suffered gearbox trouble, the 350cc Norton 'blew up expensively' (to use his own words), and in the 500cc race he finished second to Bob Anderson (Norton).

The rain that had plagued so many of the early season meetings followed the riders to Castle Combe. Mike won the two lightweight classes and mechanic Jim Adams had a rare outing, finishing second to his boss in the 250cc race riding the trusty old NSU. Mike went on to finish second in the 350 and 500cc races, being beaten in both by Minter. There was yet more shocking weather when they returned to Mallory in early May. Switching from the Mondial back to the NSU because of problems with the Italian machine, Mike won the 250cc race and then took the 350cc, beating the Scottish stars Bob McIntyre and Alistair King, both on Nortons. But positions on the starting grid were by ballot, and for the 500cc race Mike drew the back row and was never able to close the gap on his Scottish rivals, finishing third.

With the TT looming, the circus headed for two Whitsun meetings – Aberdare Park in Wales on the Saturday and Aintree on the Sunday. At Aberdare Mike had an eventful day. After winning the 125cc race he crashed in the 250cc, came back to win the 350cc, but was involved in a start-line tangle when the flag dropped for the 500. Left on the line with one leg gashed by a foot-rest, he eventually got away last but came through to finish fourth. Including heats and finals he rode in no less than seven races that day. At Aintree his little 125cc Ducati was outpaced by Chadwick's 175cc MV Agusta in the 200cc class, and he suffered engine trouble in both the 250 and 350cc before climaxing the day by winning the 500cc main

event. Then it was over to the Isle of Man for the start of TT practice.

Honda's rumoured participation had been confirmed, and *MCN* reported: 'Those Honda warriors have arrived. Four solemn faced men of the orient, the official Japanese Honda works entrants for the lightweight TT races stepped from a Dakota aircraft at Ronaldsway, Isle of Man, on Thursday afternoon.' The team's beautifully-engineered 125cc twins were much admired, and the four riders – plus their American team-manager Bill Hunt, who also rode – soon became a familiar sight buzzing round the Clypse circuit and in and out of the track-side Nursery Hotel in Onchan. However, those first-year Hondas lacked the speed of the best European bikes and it was Hailwood who made the early 125cc news when he turned out for practice on one of the brand-new twin-cylinder desmo Ducatis. Disappointingly he found it down on speed compared to the single and reverted to the older model for the race.

Whereas the previous year Mike had raced in four TTs, in 1959 he competed in five. The extra event was the so-called Formula One class for production racing machines, which opened the TT programme on Saturday 30 May. Riding a standard Manx Norton, Mike finished third at 93.73mph (150.81kph) in a three-lap race won by Alistair King on an AJS 7R, a result that underlined the steady improvement of the London-built racer compared to the Norton. For Monday's 350cc Junior TT Mike switched to Francis Beart's special lightweight Norton but was only seventh after four laps and retired with bent valves on the fifth. Both lightweight classes were run on the Clypse circuit on the Wednesday. Tarquinio Provini won the 125cc event on a works MV Agusta, snatching victory from the little Swiss Luigi Taveri, who led most of the way on a very fast East German MZ two-stroke. Mike's Ducati was not fast enough to challenge them.

Things were different in the 250cc race, where he was again up against the formidable opposition of the experienced Provini and Ubbiali, on their very swift works MV Agustas. In the race-report issue of *MCN*, I wrote: 'I don't think anyone expected Mike Hailwood, on the 1957 works Mondial, really to challenge Provini and Ubbiali on the works MVs but Mike was in absolutely brilliant form and where I was watching the race he was definitely out-riding the two Italians.' This Mondial was, in fact, the one ridden by Provini in 1957. It had been prepared by the works and flown over for Mike to race in the TT. He took the lead on the fifth lap of the ten-lap race and pulled away – only to have the magneto fail on the climb from Hillberry to Brandish during the eighth lap. Desperately disappointed, Mike looked forward to his fifth TT – the 500cc Senior on the Friday. By that time the glorious weather had changed. It was so bad that the race was postponed until the Saturday, when Mike's race-week ended with a second lap crash at Glen Tramman while holding a lowly ninth place in the rain-sodden event. Fortunately he escaped injury and, after an overnight dash, was able to race at Mallory Park the next day, where he first won the 250cc race on his own Mondial and then finished a disappointing sixth on his race-weary 350cc Norton. His bigger Norton had been too badly damaged in the TT crash to be repaired in time for Mallory.

While the Nortons were taken back to Lacey's workshop in Slough for a complete rebuild, Mike made his way to Hockenheim for the German Grand Prix the following Sunday. There he raced only in the lightweight classes, riding a works desmo Ducati single in the 125cc race and a factory-prepared Mondial single in the 250cc. In those days Hockenheim was even faster than it is today. The circuit was the shape of a fat cucumber, with an acute corner at one end and a wider-radiused one at the other, a real flat out blind where the machine was more important than the rider. In the smaller class Mike battled it out with the MV Agustas of Provini and Ubbiali, with the Ducati leading most of the way before eventually the speed of the MV Agustas told. Ubbiali won from Provini, while Mike came in third, under four seconds covering the three of them.

The 250cc race proved a disappointment. At the TT Mike's riding skill had made the two-year-old Mondial a match for the MV Agustas, but at Hockenheim it was speed that mattered, and he could only trail in fifth, well beaten not only by winner Ubbiali (MV Agusta) but by the Morinis of Emilio Mendogni and former 500cc World Champion Libero Liberati and the East German MZ two-stroke twin of Horst Fugner.

Back home, impressed by Alistair King's win in the Formula One TT, the team had acquired a 7R AJS to supplement the Norton in the 350cc class, and Mike made his AJS début at Scarborough the weekend after the German GP. He first won the 250cc race on his own Mondial and then beat AJS star Alan Shepherd in the 350cc with record laps in both events. It was typical of Mike to get the very best out of a bike first time out. Unlike most riders he did not need time to get the feel of things; he just got on a machine and rode it – 'By the seat of my pants,' as he used to say.

Mike seemed poised to win his first World Championship race when he set the fastest 125cc practice lap at the Dutch TT the next weekend, and led the race in its early stages. Then piston trouble slowed him and the race was won by Ubbiali (MV Agusta) from Bruno Spaggiari (Ducati), with Mike third. For the 250cc race MV Agusta produced brand-new twin-cylinder bikes to replace their singles, and these eventually proved too fast for the opposition led by Derek Minter (Morini) and Mike (Mondial).

From Holland the majority of riders went on to Spa for the Belgian Grand Prix the following weekend. Here Mike rode in all three solo races, which were run in a heatwave. It proved a disastrous weekend. First he retired while holding fourth place in the 125cc event when the piston of his Ducati broke. Then he pulled out of the 350cc Formula One event when his AJS gave trouble (this was particularly disappointing since he had been fastest in practice). And finally, during his Continental début in the big class his 500cc Norton slowed and he could only limp home in 13th place.

Back in England, Mike rode in three meetings in eight days (Castle Combe, Mallory Park, and Snetterton), winning seven of the 11 races he competed in, finishing second in two, third in another, and crashing in one. A significant move during this spell was that he raced a Reg Dearden Norton in the 500cc class for the first time, winning on this bike at Castle Combe. The Norton factory did not have its own team at the time but entered works bikes via Dearden; Mike's machine was a development Manx prepared by Doug Hele.

The Swedish Grand Prix at Kristianstad the next

weekend was a two-day affair which allowed Mike to race in all four classes. However, it was noteworthy on only two counts. First Mike came off his AJS during a wet practice period and suffered a gash in his nose which required five stitches; and second, because he made his début on yet another racer – a G50 Matchless in the 500cc Formula One race, in which he finished fourth. In the other races he scored a fourth and two fifths, covering a total of 380 racing miles (611.4km) over the weekend!

Back at home it was a different matter. In my *MCN* report on the British Championship meeting at Oulton Park on August Bank Holiday Monday, I wrote (under the headline 'Mike the champion'): 'Riding at his brilliant best Mike Hailwood won three of the five titles at stake.' Mike scored in the 125cc class on his Ducati, in the 250cc on a Mondial, and won the 500cc – competing against all the stars of the era – on the factory Norton. Only in the 350cc division did he fail, his AJS spluttering out with magneto trouble. The World Championship breakthrough came just five days later at the Ulster Grand Prix, when Mike won the 125cc race on a works desmo Ducati single. The task had been greatly eased by the non-participation of MV Agusta, but Mike still had to beat the very fast two-stroke MZs ridden by Ernst Degner and Gary Hocking. In fact Hocking, on the bigger MZ, won the 250cc class ahead of Mike on his Mondial.

Three meetings in England followed in quick succession – Aberdare Park, Silverstone, and Oulton Park. Mike rode in 12 finals, won seven of them, and was second twice. Then it was over to Italy for the Grand Prix at Monza, where he accepted an invitation from the gifted East German engineer Walter Kaaden to race an MZ two-stroke twin in the 250cc class. Mike held fourth place early in the race but then had to make a pit stop to replace the gear pedal, which had fallen off. This dropped him to 20th, but he recovered to finish ninth in a race won by Ubbiali (MV Agusta), who beat Ernst Degner (MZ) by just half a wheel. Earlier Degner had won the 125cc class on his smaller MZ, Mike's Ducati being outclassed (he struggled home eighth). In his third race, the 500cc, Mike's Norton suffered valve-gear problems while he was dicing for third place with

Duke (Norton), Dickie Dale (BMW), and Bob Brown (Norton).

The season then finished with the usual hectic round of British events. Mike raced at seven very different circuits in the space of just four weeks. Excluding the qualifying heats that were run at some events, he rode in 28 races on five different bikes (he used both Norton and AJS in the 350cc events) and won 17 of them. At the end he was confirmed as the clear-cut winner of all four ACU Road Racing Stars, and in mid-October I was privileged to be the only journalist invited to try four of the bikes at Brands Hatch. The idea was to not only give me a chance to ride the very best of racing machinery but also to find out just how it felt to jump from one to another as Mike did at meeting after meeting. The four machines in question were the 125cc Ducati, 250cc Mondial, 350cc AJS, and 500cc Norton. The experience was certainly an eye-opener and proved to me just what a natural Mike was, to get the very best out of a tiny lightweight that revved to 13,000 and then, within minutes, to be racing a thundering Manx Norton where anything over 8,000 revs would result in tangled valves. In the issue of *MCN* that carried my report of this outing, I wrote: 'Mike wins so many races and breaks so many records that his name inevitably appears in our columns week after week until we begin to take this phenomenal rider for granted.' The incredible fact was that he was still only 19 years old!

In two-and-a-half years of almost non-stop racing he had won well over 100 races and broken over 50 lap and race records. Perhaps unsurprisingly under such circumstances, this year he decided not to go racing in South Africa, but took a break instead.

Scarborough, September 1958, and Mike (Norton) leads the 350cc field from the start, masking Geoff Duke (Norton), whose helmet can be seen above his. On the right is Ralph Rensen (Norton), and on the left Alan Holmes (Norton). Mike won. (B.R. Nicholls)

Left This classic shot at Mere Hairpin shows Mike in winning action on his 350cc Norton at Scarborough in September 1958, when he beat a star-studded field. (B.R. Nicholls)

Right There is a wintry look about this picture of Mike on his 350cc Norton at the Crystal Palace track in South London in October 1958. Despite the rain he won all four solo races. (B.R. Nicholls)

Below Mike's first appearance in Mallory Park's famous 'Race of the Year' was in September 1958. Winner John Surtees (MV Agusta) gets away first ahead of Bob McIntyre (Norton), with Hailwood (Norton, 4), Bob Anderson (Norton, 5), Derek Minter (Norton, 6), and Alistair King (Norton, 7) completing a numerically neat front row. (B.R. Nicholls)

Far right Spring 1959 at Brands Hatch, and Mike is at the Kent track to test-ride a 175cc twin-cylinder racer that the Ducati factory had sent over for evaluation. He never raced this bike, but it lead to the development of the 250 and 350cc Ducati twins. (Mick Woollett)

Below right Action at Whitegates corner on the outskirts of Ramsey as Mike cranks his Beart-prepared Norton into the left-hander during the 1959 Junior TT. He retired with valve problems. (B.R. Nicholls)

Left *The twin-cylinder 125cc Ducati was not a success. Here Mike on the twin chases Bruno Spaggiari on a single-cylinder Ducati during practice for the 1959 Lightweight TT. He reverted to a single for the race.* (B.R. Nicholls)

Below left *Mike (Ducati) just beats Carlo Ubbiali (MV Agusta) away at the start of the 1959 125cc Lightweight TT ahead of race-winner Tarquinio Provini (MV Agusta, 5). Massed starts were a feature of races held on the Clypse circuit.* (Don Morley)

Right *Italian Tarquinio Provini on a works MV Agusta leads Mike (Mondial) on the Clypse circuit during the 1959 250cc TT. Mike took the lead and looked set to win until ignition failure ruled him out.* (B.R. Nicholls)

Below *Start of the 125cc German Grand Prix at Hockenheim in 1959 and Mike, in the front row (Ducati, 147), gets away. He finished third behind Carlo Ubbiali (MV Agusta, 152) and Tarquinio Provini (MV Agusta, 151).* (Mick Woollett)

Above left *Tension at the start of the 1959 125cc Dutch TT as Mike (Ducati, 4), Ernst Degner (MZ), and Tarquinio Provini (MV Agusta) keep their eyes on the starter. Mike led most of the way but was then slowed by piston trouble and finished third.* (Mick Woollett)

Left *Mike lunges forward (Ducati, 4) as the starter of the 1959 125cc Belgian Grand Prix drops the flag. But his race ended with piston failure. The winner was Carlo Ubbiali (MV Agusta, 16). Others in the picture are Derek Minter (MZ, 2), Bruno Spaggiari (Ducati, 10), and Luigi Taveri (Ducati, 8).* (Mick Woollett)

Above *Three famous names dicing in the 350cc class of the 1959 Swedish Grand Prix at Kristianstad, with Australian Ken Kavanagh (Norton) leading Dickie Dale (AJS) and Mike (AJS).* (Mick Woollett)

Right *The Ulster Grand Prix on the Dundrod circuit in August 1959. Bob McIntyre (AJS) leads similarly-mounted Mike in the 350cc race. Both retired.* (B.R. Nicholls)

Above far left *Heading for his first World Championship win Mike (Ducati) chases Rhodesian Gary Hocking (MZ) during the 1959 125cc Ulster Grand Prix.* (B.R. Nicholls)

Left *Celebrations after his first Grand Prix win. Mike (centre) flanked by runner-up Gary Hocking (right) and third-placed Ernst Degner after his winning ride in the 1959 125cc Ulster Grand Prix.* (B.R. Nicholls)

Above left *Another shot from the 1959 Ulster Grand Prix – this time with the winner's garland, the race-winning 125cc Ducati, and Ducati mechanic Oscar Polesani.* (B.R. Nicholls)

Above *Action from Aberdare Park in Wales as Mike (nearest camera), Alan Trow, Dan Shorey and Eric Hinton prepare to push their Manx Nortons into life in August 1959. Mike came first.* (Mick Woollett)

Right *Mike's occasional rides on the East German MZ two-strokes started with the 250cc class of the Italian Grand Prix at Monza in 1959, where he is seen trying the bike for size. He finished ninth in the race after a long pit-stop to replace the gear pedal.* (Mick Woollett)

Above left *Scotland's Bob McIntyre (AJS) leads Mike (Norton) in the 350cc race at Mallory Park in September 1959. Bob won from Mike and they shared a new lap record at 85.87mph (138.16kph).* (B.R. Nicholls)

Left *Against a backdrop of massed spectators Mike heads for third place in Mallory Park's 'Race of the Year' in September 1959 on his 500cc Norton.* (B.R. Nicholls)

Above *Clowning it up at Mallory Park's 'Race of the Year' meeting in September 1959. Left to right: John Lewis, circuit owner Clive Wormleighton, Ginger Payne, Bob Anderson, Paddy Driver, and Mike. The riders are celebrating getting their prize-money cheques.* (B.R. Nicholls)

Right *Mike sets out on a lap of honour after winning the 250cc race at Mallory Park in September 1959.* (B.R. Nicholls)

CHAPTER 3

Eleven out of twelve

The start of the 1960s was a boom time for motorcycle sport and bike sales in Britain. Double World Champion John Surtees had just been voted the country's top sportsman in both the BBC Sportsman of the Year poll and by the Sports Writers' Association; sales of motorcycles had reached almost 300,000 in 1959 (*double* the previous year's figure); and sales of *MCN*, the paper I worked for at the time, had increased from a few thousand to over 60,000 in just three years.

Travelling was easier too. Minister of Transport Ernest Marples had opened what is widely (but not entirely accurately) regarded as Britain's first motorway, the M1, on 2 November 1959, saying: 'We must press on – we must create a road system worthy of the third quarter of the twentieth century. There is no earthly reason why we should fail.' (For the record, the eight-mile/12.9km Preston bypass was Britain's first official

Mike drifts his Norton round Stowe Corner during his winning ride in the 500cc class of the international meeting at Silverstone in late May 1960. During the race he clocked the first-ever 100mph (161kph) lap of the circuit on a motorcycle, at 100.16mph (161.16kph). (B.R. Nicholls)

motorway.) Mr Marples' words mirrored the optimism of the nation as we faced a new decade. However, he also observed that: 'On this magnificent road the speed which can easily be reached is so great that senses may be numbed and judgement warped. The margin of error gets smaller as the speeds get faster'. Indeed, in those days there was no upper speed limit at all on the M1 or other unrestricted roads.

On the Hailwood front, Mike was considering his own future. In *MCN* I reported that Mike had told me he felt that competing in all four classes was just a bit too much, and that jumping straight from the little 125cc Ducati on to his big Norton was asking for trouble. However, he did not rule out racing a works 125cc in the classics. He had a fruitless journey to Italy in February 1960, when he flew out to test Ducati's first 250cc racer, only to find that it was not ready. This meant that he had to go back later in the month, when I reported in *MCN*: 'Last week Mike Hailwood and Ducati tester Franco Farne both tried the new 250cc twin-cylinder desmo Ducati that has been built to order for the Hailwood equipe. The tests took place at Modena and Mike expressed complete satisfaction with the first outing.'

Just how much money Stan Hailwood put into this project is not known, but it was certainly he who persuaded the Italian factory to design and build a 'doubled-up' version of their successful 125cc racer. The new machine had the same bore and stroke (55.3 x 52mm), produced around 43bhp, revved to 11,600, and had a top speed of about 130mph (209kph). At the end of March the British Motor Cycle Racing Club organised a practice day at Silverstone and Mike took advantage of this to try out his 1960 bikes, including a brand-new 350cc Norton which had been prepared by Francis Beart, a 350cc special consisting of a 7R AJS engine in a Norton frame, his faithful old 250cc Mondial, the new 250cc Ducati, and a 500cc Norton.

The season opened at the same circuit on 9 April with the international Hutchinson 100. Mike had a great day, scoring two wins and two hard-fought second places. The wins came in the 125 and 250cc races, the new Ducati making a sensational début which included breaking the 250cc lap record at 91.43mph (147.11kph), the only new solo lap record to be set that day. In the 350cc race Mike rode his AJS and was beaten by half a second by Bob McIntyre (AJS), while Frank Perris – later Mike's partner in Perwood Homes (a building company in South Africa) – pipped him in the 500cc class by a wheel, both riding Nortons. The day ended perfectly for the Hailwood equipe when it was announced that Mike had won the Mellano Trophy, calculated on a complicated formula involving race speeds, for his performance on the bigger Ducati.

Silverstone was followed by no less than nine meetings on eight different British circuits in the space of a month, starting at Brands Hatch on 15 April and ending at the same circuit on 15 May. At these Mike scored 21 wins and six second places, as well as crashing twice. The main lesson learned was that while the 250cc Ducati was fast and competitive on quick circuits like Silverstone, it did not handle well on the shorter, trickier courses on which the majority of races were held. So after the third of the nine meetings, Mike reverted to his four-year-old Mondial for the 250 class. When I visited Mike and his two mechanics at their Oxford workshop I was told that the Ducati had been sent back to Italy for a new frame to be fitted. I was also told that the experi-

ment of fitting a 7R AJS engine in a Norton frame was not a success. But on the positive side, Mike was delighted with the improved 125cc model which Ducati had built during the winter, and which had carried him to nine straight wins.

The day after Brands Hatch, the last of the early season meetings, Mike flew out to Italy to try the 250cc Ducati with its new frame. There were also rumours that Stan had persuaded the factory's talented technical boss Fabio Taglioni to build a 350cc version, and that Mike would be trying this out too. Sure enough, Mike arrived back for a major international at Silverstone accompanied by a 350cc, but it handled so badly during practice that he was forced to revert to his AJS for the race. He won both the lightweight classes on the smaller Ducatis; retired from the 350cc when his AJS seized, and then caused a sensation when he not only won the 500cc class but became the first rider ever to lap the famous circuit at over 100mph (161kph). Reporting the meeting for *MCN* under the front page headline 'Mike tops the ton', I wrote: 'Mike Hailwood, unchallenged king of the lightweights, shook even his most ardent admirers when he rocketed away to win the 500cc class of the International meeting at Silverstone on Saturday. None of the star-studded entry could stay with the 20-year-old Oxford flyer … who shattered the Silverstone motorcycle lap record with a lap at 100.16mph [161.16kph].' In fact the engine was a Norton unit prepared not by Lacey but by rival Francis Beart, who had replaced the standard single plug ignition system with a twin-plug set-up. He had also prepared the AJS that Mike rode at Silverstone.

The next race on the calendar was the Isle of Man TT and life was made simpler by the fact that the organisers had abandoned the short Clypse circuit and all races were run over the traditional 37.7-mile (60.66km) Mountain course. The Hailwood camp was now overflowing with Ducatis, for Stan had bought all three of the desmo 125cc twins, which had proved disappointing the previous season, to supplement the improved single, plus the 250 and 350cc twins. During practice Mike established that the twin was slower than the single and that neither of the bigger twins handled well. He decided to start on the 250 but ditched the larger in favour of his AJS. However, all three classes proved to be disasters. Mike crashed in the 125cc race on the first lap, then retired on the opening lap of the 250cc event when first the throttle jammed and then the throttle cable broke at Sulby. Finally the AJS gave trouble: petrol siphoning through the breather forced an early pit stop, and then the carburettor came loose.

Three races – three retirements. The Hailwood camp was not a happy one. However, they cheered up on the Friday of race-week when Mike finished an impressive third in the 500cc Senior TT, beaten only by the far faster works MV Agusta four-cylinder racers ridden by the two Johns – Surtees and Hartle. Mike averaged 98.29mph (158.15kph) for the seven-lap, 226-mile (363.63km) race – the best-ever figure achieved by a single-cylinder machine – and lapped at 100.37mph (161.5kph). He just missed out on being the first to lap the TT circuit at over a ton on a single – that honour went to Derek Minter, who got round at 101.05mph (162.59kph) on his Steve Lancefield Norton just seconds ahead of Mike, only to retire with a split oil tank. At the award ceremony that evening Norman Dixon, head of the organising committee, presented Minter with a cheque for £100 pledged by Stan Hailwood the previous year for the first to lap at 100mph (161kph) on a single – a prize which was so nearly won by his son!

Tiring of ignition problems with the 350cc AJS, the team replaced the normal magneto with a battery and coil system for the post-TT Mallory Park meeting. This proved a success, with Mike winning from Bob McIntyre on his AJS with special frame, though the tough Scot turned the tables in the 500cc class in which he came from behind to beat Mike, both men this time on Nortons.

The Continental classics started with the Dutch TT, where Mike competed in three classes but had a poor day. The 125cc is noteworthy because Jim Redman, who went on to win six World Championships, made his début on a works Honda. However, the Japanese bikes were still not competitive and he finished only fourth, though still well ahead of Mike, who struggled home eighth on a Ducati single. Mike then took fifth place on his Mondial in the 250cc class, and also came

fifth in the 500cc when his Norton suffered a split petrol tank and a loose foot-rest and then slowed during the final laps. When Beart later stripped the engine he found that the timing side crankcase had cracked in half.

Things were brighter at the Belgian Grand Prix the next weekend. The single-cylinder Ducati and the ageing Mondial had been replaced by a pair of Ducati twins for the lightweight classes. In the smaller class Mike finished sixth behind the works MZs and MV Agustas, ahead of all the Hondas, and in the 250cc race he was fourth, beaten only by the works MV Agustas. He ended his day with fourth place in the 500cc race behind Surtees and Hartle on their MV Agustas and Australian Bob Brown on a Norton.

Back in England the first meeting on the new long circuit at Brands Hatch, an international event, was held six days after the Belgian. Here, despite pouring rain, Mike won all four solo classes, a stunning performance in conditions in which he hated racing. A week later Mike nearly repeated the dose at Castle Combe, but a missed gear resulted in bent valves which dropped him and his AJS to third place in the 350cc race. At Mallory the next day there was, as usual, no 125cc class, but he won the 250, limped home fifth in the 350cc on the hastily repaired AJS, and finished the day by beating McIntyre in the all-important 500cc event. At the time, Mike was again talking of giving up the 125cc class. I wrote in *MCN*: 'For some time now Mike has found that riding the tiddlers has been spoiling his technique on the bigger models.' I also hinted that Mike, with the energetic backing of his father, was actively campaigning for a ride on the big MV Agustas, spurred on by rumours that John Surtees was to retire from bikes at the end of the season.

After meetings at Snetterton and Oulton Park at which he scored five wins from ten starts, including one on the 250cc Ducati, which had been fitted with a new frame (made by Ernie Earles in England), Mike crossed to Ireland for the Ulster Grand Prix. Again a classic meeting proved a disappointment. The bikes were good enough to win in England, but not when up against factory opposition. As a result his best placing was fourth in the 250cc on the revamped Ducati, beaten by winner Ubbiali (MV Agusta) and by the fast-improving four-cylinder Hondas, ridden by Tom Phillis and Jim Redman.

Returning to England, Mike won all three races he contested at Aberdare. The very next weekend he thrilled the crowd at Brands Hatch when, after crashing at over 70mph (113kph) in the 500cc final while chasing Minter, he jumped up, remounted, and finished third. I commented in *MCN* that this was 'the most fantastic performance of a brilliant day's racing', for Mike had earlier won the 200cc race on his Ducati, beating Phillis on a works Honda; the 250cc back on his old Mondial; and the 350cc on an AJS.

After a meeting of mixed fortunes at Snetterton, a track where he usually did well, Mike set out for the Italian Grand Prix at Monza, where Morini let him try one of their works 250cc singles during an early practice session. He felt he had done reasonably well, but after promising to tailor the bike to fit him the team left Monza and never returned. Mike reverted to his Ducati for the race, but the bike had already proved slow in practice and he retired with a misfire. On the bigger Ducati twin he had been fifth fastest in practice, but in the race the rear wheel collapsed. Only in the 500cc race did things go well when his Norton carried him to third place behind the MV Agustas of Surtees and Emilio Mendogni.

The long hard season was telling on the bikes and mechanics. Consequently Mike withdrew from the mid-September Scarborough meeting, preferring to get things right in preparation for the Brands Hatch meeting on Sunday 18 September, where he won four of the five classes contested. His only defeat came in the smallest class at the hands of Phillis on his works Honda, but he turned the tables on the Japanese team in the 250cc race when he rode his old Mondial to victory ahead of Redman on a four-cylinder Honda.

The next weekend was a busy one, with a meeting at Aintree on the Saturday and the 'Race of the Year' at Mallory the next day. Aintree is noteworthy because Mike did not win a single race, scoring just three second places and a third. But the 250cc race was an historic one because McIntyre, riding a Honda four, scored the Japanese factory's first 250cc win in Europe, beating

Mike and the old Mondial after what was described as a titanic battle. At Mallory Mike had the most profitable day of his career so far when he won the £1,000 first prize 'Race of the Year' ahead of Terry Shepherd (Norton) and Ron Langston (Matchless), after what I described in my report in *MCN* as 'one of the most thrilling races ever seen at the Leicestershire track. During the race Mike set a new lap record at 89.00mph [143.2kph].' Even so, not all spectators were happy. Two *MCN* readers wrote in to complain about the ten-shilling (50p) admission charge, which equates to perhaps £10 today.

Not surprisingly, it was at about this time that rumours linking Mike with a possible Honda ride for the 1961 season began to spread. In my Paddock Gossip column in *MCN* in late September I wrote: 'I can tell you Mike Hailwood is very interested [in a Honda ride] and don't be surprised if he visits Japan in the near future.' I also noted that Mike had scored an unbroken run of 41 successive wins in the 250cc class of mainland meetings on his Mondial until beaten by McIntyre and the Honda at Aintree – statistics no doubt supplied by Stan. After rain-sodden meetings at Oulton Park and Brands Hatch in early October, at which Mike scored two wins, including another over Redman on the Honda four, Mike and mechanic Jim Adams headed off to Spain for a bit of sunshine, rest, and relaxation. There he competed in both solo classes at Zaragoza, winning the 125cc on a Ducati and the 500cc on a Norton.

Mike had again won all four ACU Road Racing Stars to bring his total to 11 out of 12 of these awards in the past three years, confirming his position as the most successful British rider of all time. However, all this success was perhaps just too much for the British public, for despite having been runner-up in the annual *MCN* Man of the Year contest on two previous occasions he dropped to third in the 1960 poll, beaten by moto-cross star Dave Bickers and retiring double World Champion John Surtees.

The first big news of 1961 came in mid-January, when Count Domenico Agusta, whose bikes had won all four solo World Championships in 1960, decided to quit racing with immediate effect. He claimed that supporting the ever-growing number of championship races was simply costing him too much money. For the autocratic Count, racing had always been more of a hobby than a commercial enterprise. The motorcycle manufacturing side of MV Agusta was tiny compared to its helicopter production, and obviously the cost of combating the rising tide of the Honda challenge and the retirement of his two great champions, John Surtees and Carlo Ubbiali, had focused his mind. The Count's decision obviously ruled out any chance Mike may have had of joining MV Agusta for 1961 and left the team looking elsewhere for top-class machinery. One minor coup was that Stan persuaded Mondial to sell him a 1957 works machine, said to be the one raced by Tarquinio Provini, to replace the 1956 model that Mike had raced with amazing success for two years. But this would obviously be no match for the increasingly successful four-cylinder Hondas in the classic events.

Leaving Stan to battle with this problem, Mike and his great friend and rival Tony Godfrey left, at very short notice, to race in America. They had been invited to compete in the US Grand Prix at Daytona, an FIM-sanctioned event run by a small organisation set up in opposition to the mighty American Motorcycle Association, which was not, at that time, part of the FIM. The organisers had contacted the Hailwood equipe to give some world-wide credibility to the event, and within days Mike and Tony were en route from Southampton to New York by transatlantic liner. They took with them Mike's 250cc Mondial and 500cc Norton and a G50 Matchless that Tony had borrowed from London dealer Geoff Monty. Rough seas delayed them by a day and forced them to fly down to Daytona rather than taking a train as originally planned. At Daytona, Mike finished second on the Mondial, beaten by Moto Kitano on a four-cylinder Honda, while Tony won the 500cc class on the borrowed Matchless, Mike retiring with ignition trouble. Mike later told me he had been impressed by the enthusiasm of the Americans, though he had been startled by the coloured leathers some of them wore – all European riders wore sober, tight-fitting black riding suits at that time.

While he had been away mechanic Jim Adams had been out testing the 350cc Ducati twin, which was now fitted with a leading link Reynolds fork. Then in March there was a strong rumour that Mike would join Alan Shepherd in the East German MZ team. Mike had a good relationship with MZ technical boss Walter Kaaden and had ridden a 250cc MZ twin at Monza in 1959. In fact he did fly out to the factory at Zshopau to try the bikes, but the big stumbling block was finance – the East Germans were desperately short of 'hard' Western currency and could not afford even a meagre retainer.

Behind the scenes Stan was scheming to get Mike a Honda ride, and in *MCN*'s Paddock Gossip column in March I wrote: 'I've got a hunch that we'll be seeing Mike on a Honda in the 250cc class this year. The big problem is that Honda are on Castrol oil while Mike is a Shell/BP runner.' In those days a rider's main source of income came from the oil companies, and only a year earlier John Hartle's plan to join Honda had been scuppered because his oil company refused to let him ride a Castrol-lubricated machine. How could the Hailwoods get round this problem? After a great deal of political manoeuvring Honda agreed to lend three 250cc machines to the British importer and these would be raced by Mike, McIntyre, and Minter in competition with the official works team of Redman, Phillis, and Kunimitsu Takahashi.

By the time this was settled the season was already under way. Mike's programme started with five British meetings – Brands Hatch, Snetterton, Thruxton, Silverstone, and Mallory Park – in the space of ten days. He rode in 16 finals and won 11 of them. His most successful day was at Thruxton, where, in a meeting televised by the BBC, he won six races – three heats and three finals. The least profitable was Silverstone, where he was disqualified while leading on his Ducati because he had entered on a Mondial, and had to retire with machine troubles from both the 350cc and 500cc races, in which he rode an AJS and a Norton with an experimental one-piece crank.

At the first classic of 1961 there was no Honda for Mike to ride, so he took the 1957 Mondial and, because the Honda arrangement covered only the 250cc class, he accepted the offer of one of Joe Ehrlich's British-built single-cylinder two-strokes for the 125cc race. The impact of this new pairing was immediate. Round the twists and turns of the tricky Montjuich Park circuit overlooking Barcelona, Mike was in a class of his own. Tearing ahead from the start, he built up a half-minute lead over the pursuing works Hondas and MZs, only to have the vital exhaust expansion chamber split. This slowed the EMC substantially, and Mike limped home fourth, with Phillis (Honda) the winner from Ernst Degner (MZ) and Redman (Honda). He was never in the picture in the 250cc race. The Mondial was slow to start, and he eventually retired after crashing and remounting. However, the race was notable because Count Agusta had relented on his strict 'no race' policy and had agreed to supply existing bikes for Rhodesian Gary Hocking to race in some events – and it was Hocking on an MV Agusta twin who won.

It proved a lone 250cc success, for while Hocking concentrated on winning the 350 and 500cc World Championships, Honda won the ten remaining 250cc classic races. Mike had his first outing on a Honda at Brands Hatch the weekend after the Spanish. His mount was a 1960 bike, and despite the fact that it was his first-ever race on a four-cylinder machine, he won at an average speed faster than his old lap record! The next two classics were the German Grand Prix at Hockenheim and the French at Clermont-Ferrand the following weekend in May. In Germany, Mike rode the year-old Honda and could only struggle home eighth, outpaced by the 1961 Hondas, the lone works Morini, and the MZ two-stroke twins. In the 125cc class he again raced an EMC but engine trouble forced his retirement. His best placing was in the 500cc race, where he came fourth behind Hocking, Perris (Norton), and Hans-Gunther Jager (BMW).

The flat-out nature of Hockenheim meant that riding skill counted for little – but it was a different matter at the hilly and sinuous Clermont-Ferrand circuit the following Sunday. Despite the fact that he was still on the old bike Mike was fastest in practice, ahead of the official works team. Hocking led in the early stages on the MV Agusta twin, only to retire, and it was Phillis who won with Mike second. Mike also finished fourth on the 125cc EMC and came a splendid second to Hocking in the 500cc race. He then returned home to prepare for the TT. He raced at Castle Combe, winning on the 250cc Honda and his 500cc Norton, before crossing to the Isle of Man, where he had been promised a new Honda for the 250cc race and a 125cc for the smaller capacity class.

The 1961 TT proved a triumph for Hailwood. First he scored a lightweight double on the opening day when he won the 125 and 250cc races on Hondas at record speeds. Then he finished the week by winning the 500cc Senior TT on his Norton at an average speed of 100.60mph (161.87kph) – the first time a single cylinder machine had averaged over a ton, and the first British win since Ray Amm had scored a controversial success on a Norton in a rain-sodden, shortened race in 1954. The Norton had been built for Mike by Bill Lacey in his Slough workshop and non-standard features included the one-piece crank assembly, twin-plug ignition, and an Italian Oldani front brake. A five-speed gearbox was also tried, but a standard four-speeder was fitted for the race. Only in the mid-week 350cc Junior TT did Mike fail, and even then it was a glorious failure. For he took the lead when Hocking's far-faster four-cylinder MV Agusta began to slow and looked to have the race won when he started the last lap comfortably ahead of Phil Read (Norton). But at Milntown, approaching Ramsey, and with just 14 miles (22.5km) of the 226-mile (363.63km) race to go, the gudgeon pin of his 7R broke.

It had been a truly sensational week for the Hailwood equipe. Mike had won his first TT, and had then become the first man ever to win three TTs in a week. These successes meant that he now led the 500cc World Championship and had also emerged as a serious challenger in the 250cc class. He had served his apprenticeship, and had now seized the opportunity to succeed at the very highest level of motorcycle racing.

Mike with winner's garland after one of his three wins at the Silverstone international meeting in late May 1960. (B.R. Nicholls)

Left *Typical short-circuit action as Derek Minter (Norton) leads Mike (Norton) at Brands Hatch in April 1960. Minter won both the big bike races that day, with Mike – who won the two lightweight classes – second in both.* (B.R. Nicholls)

Below left *Druid's Hill at Brands Hatch, May 1960, and Mike (Mondial, 144) takes a wide line as he chases Mike O'Rourke (Ariel) in the 250cc race. Mike won, breaking both race and lap records.* (B.R. Nicholls)

Right *During 1960 Mike experimented with a form of disc brake. Here, wearing a hat, he discusses the project with South African Paddy Driver.* (Mick Woollett)

Below *Action at Ginger Hall during the 1960 Junior TT as Mike accelerates out of the left-hander on his AJS. He later retired with carburettor problems.* (B.R. Nicholls)

Above *Just two days after finishing third in the 1960 500cc Senior TT on a Norton Mike was in action again at Mallory Park. Here he is pictured winning the 350cc race on his AJS.* (B.R. Nicholls)

Above right *A streaming wet track at Brands Hatch in July 1960, but Mike won all four main solo classes. Here he is in action on his 350cc AJS.* (B.R. Nicholls)

Below *The 250cc Ducati twin that Mike raced occasionally during the 1960 season was fast but did not handle as well as his Mondial. The picture shows him winning on the Ducati at Oulton Park in August 1960.* (B.R. Nicholls)

Opposite top *Fast starter Mike (AJS) leads the 350cc field up to Druids at Brands Hatch in August 1960. He won this race and two others at this meeting.* (B.R. Nicholls)

Opposite below *Despite works opposition in the form of Australian Tom Phillis on his Honda twin (left) Mike still won the 200cc class at Brands Hatch in August 1960 on his single-cylinder Ducati.* (B.R. Nicholls)

Below *Oulton Park promoter Rex Foster congratulates Mike in August 1960 after a hard day's racing during which he won two British Championships and finished second in the other two!* (B.R. Nicholls)

Above *Classic action at Brands Hatch in August 1960 as 'King of Brands' Derek Minter (Norton) leads Mike (Norton) in the 500cc race. Minter won both big bike races that day with Mike second in one and third in the other after crashing and remounting.* (B.R. Nicholls)

Left *During practising for the Italian Grand Prix at Monza in 1960 Mike tried a works Morini, but he reverted to his Ducati twin for the 250cc race. As he takes off his helmet he discusses the bike with Bill Webster and Morini's race-chief Dante Lambertini, while mechanic Elio Albertazzi (right) looks on.* (Carlo Perelli)

Above right *Dicing with South African Paddy Driver (Norton) at the Mallory Park 'Race of the Year' in September 1960, Mike (Norton) takes the outside line as they sweep round Gerrard's Bend. Mike went on to win.* (B.R. Nicholls)

Right *A youthful Murray Walker (left) interviews Mike and Derek Minter after the September 1960 meeting at Brands Hatch, during which Mike had twice beaten Minter.* (B.R. Nicholls)

Far right *Mike looks relaxed after winning the 'Race of the Year' at Mallory Park in September 1960. Celebrating with him are his father Stan, centre, and mechanic Jim Adams.* (B.R. Nicholls)

Above *Early in 1961 Mike (second left) went to East Germany at the invitation of MZ to try their 125 and 250cc racers. Here he poses with MZ technical boss Walter Kaaden, Alan Shepherd, Ernst Degner, and Hans Fischer.* (Mick Woollett)

Left *Twenty-one today! Stan Hailwood hands Mike the key of the door as they celebrate his coming of age at Snetterton on 2 April 1961. Mike won two of his three races that day and finished second in the other.* (B.R. Nicholls)

Above right *During 1961 Mike carried out a lot of tests with the new 350cc twin-cylinder Ducati in an attempt to improve the handling. He is seen here trying it with a Reynolds leading-link fork at Silverstone.* (Mick Woollett)

Right *Flat on the tank and heading for his first TT win, Mike in action on a works Honda twin in the 1961 125cc Lightweight TT at Stella Maris on the way out of Ramsey. It was his first ride on a 125cc Honda.* (B.R. Nicholls)

Above *Multiple handshakes after the 1961 250cc TT from the riders who took the first three places. Winner Mike (centre) is congratulated by runner-up Bob McIntyre (right) and Australian Tom Phillis. All three rode four-cylinder Hondas.* (B.R. Nicholls)

Left *Cranking the 250cc four-cylinder Honda round Quarter Bridge, Mike sets out to complete a TT double win on Monday, 12 June 1961, having already won the 125cc race in the morning.* (B.R. Nicholls)

Right *A proud father-and-son team with the two TT trophies at the presentation ceremony at the Villa Marina, Douglas, on the evening of Mike's double TT win on Monday, 12 June 1961.* (B.R. Nicholls)

Left *Rem Fowler, who won the twin-cylinder class of the first TT back in 1907, chats to Mike during his record-breaking 1961 TT week in which he won three TTs.* (B.R. Nicholls)

Right *Completing a marvellous 1961 TT week, Mike hurls his Bill Lacey-tuned 500cc Norton into Signpost Corner on his way to winning the Senior TT, his third victory of the week.* (B.R. Nicholls)

Below *Impromptu press conference after Mike's 1961 Senior TT win. Left to right: Peter Arnold (smoking), Harry Louis (in hat) and Charlie Rous.* (B.R. Nicholls)

CHAPTER 4

The first World Championship

The battle for the 250cc World Championship was on. Mike's win at the TT had elevated him to joint third place with Jim Redman (both on 14 points), behind Kunimitsu Takahashi with 15 points and Tom Phillis with 20. If he could do well in the next classic, the Dutch TT, he would be in with a real chance of winning his first world title at the age of 21.

In the event – which was the first race in the day-long programme, watched by the usual 150,000 crowd – Mike simply pulverised the opposition. Taking the lead from the start, he left Bob McIntyre, Redman, and Phillis trailing, to win by a clear half-minute, slicing five seconds off the old lap record as he went. With previous leader Phillis retiring and Redman coming only third, this success leapfrogged Mike into the lead with 22 points to Phillis's 20 and Redman's 18. Later in the day Mike slid off his 125cc Honda when forced off-line by a lapped rider as he

The chase is on. Mike on his four-cylinder Honda could not catch Bob McIntyre (Honda) in the 250cc 1961 Ulster Grand Prix, but a second place consolidated his World Championship lead ahead of Honda teamsters Jim Redman and Tom Phillis. (B.R. Nicholls)

was dicing for the lead with Phillis, but he ended the day on a high note by taking second place on his Norton in the 500cc class after pushing Hocking on the MV Agusta all the way. This win put Hocking back in the lead in the 500cc championship by a single point, 24 to 23. However, Mike knew he had no real chance of taking the 500cc title because the four-cylinder MV Agusta was just too fast. His main aim was to win the 250cc crown.

Heatwave weather greeted us at the Belgian Grand Prix the following weekend, where Mike set the pace during 250cc practice. But on the ultra-fast Spa-Francorchamps circuit the bikes of the factory riders proved faster, and Redman won from Phillis with Hailwood, who was never in the hunt, a distant third. His 125cc outing was again disappointing. The little Honda gave trouble and he retired at the pits, but, as in Holland, the day ended well with another second place behind Hocking, who set a sizzling lap record at 123.48mph (198.68kph) on his MV Agusta. Mike averaged 116.69mph (187.75kph) and the team were relieved to see the chequered flag, because Bill Lacey had spent all night rebuilding the engine after it had failed during the final practice session.

The position in the 250cc title chase was now intriguing, for Mike shared the lead with Phillis and Redman, all with 26 points. I wrote in *MCN*'s Paddock Gossip: 'This is a real battle for the Honda company have no control over Mike's riding at all – they simply supply the machines and that's that ... and the same applies to Bob McIntyre and John Hartle' – Hartle having replaced Minter on the third 'British' Honda.

After a brief trip back to England to compete at Brands Hatch and Castle Combe, scoring three wins in six starts, the team left for the long haul to the Sachsenring for the East German Grand Prix. Again on a circuit that demanded riding skill rather than sheer speed, Hailwood was outstanding. Watched by a crowd of a quarter-million sport-starved East Germans, he shattered the lap record and won the 250cc race, easing up ahead of Redman, Takahashi, and Phillis on the official works Hondas. This success broke the three-way championship tie and put him ahead, with 34 points to Redman's 32 and Phillis's 29. Once again the 125cc Honda gave trouble, Mike retiring after a pit-stop to change plugs had failed to cure the problem, but, repeating the pattern set in Holland and Belgium, his big Norton carried him to second place behind Hocking in the 500cc race. Back home, meanwhile, Stan had been having a clear out, selling all three desmo Ducati twins (two 250 and one 350cc) to John Surtees – the smaller machines because they were now surplus to requirements and the 350cc because the team simply could not get it to handle and Mike preferred to race the AJS.

En route to the Ulster Grand Prix they took in the August Bank Holiday meeting at Oulton Park, where Mike just beat Hartle in the 250cc race (both Honda-mounted) but failed to shine in the larger classes; retiring from the 350cc with carburettor trouble and finishing only third in the 500cc – a poor performance by his high standards. In Ulster he did not win the all-important 250cc race but did consolidate his championship lead by finishing second behind McIntyre – always at his brilliant best on genuine road circuits – ahead of Redman and Phillis. He now had 40 points, five ahead of Redman and eight in front of Phillis. With just three rounds to go his grip on the title was tightening.

For the first race in four outings his 125cc Honda kept going, but with no chance of doing well in the championship Mike was happy to finish a relaxed fifth in a race won by Takahashi (Honda) from Degner (MZ). In the 500cc race he was again outstanding, finishing second to Hocking for the fifth time, though hard-pressed by Alistair King (Norton), who finished just one second behind Mike. All these 500cc successes, plus his prowess on the 250cc Honda, had meanwhile caught the eye of Count Domenico Agusta, and the week after the Ulster Grand Prix *MCN* carried a front page story that rumours emanating from both Italy and England 'indicate that Mike Hailwood may be mounted on works MV Agustas for both the 350 and 500cc classes of the Italian Grand Prix at Monza on Sunday, September 3.'

Honouring home commitments, Mike raced at Brands Hatch – winning the 350cc race on his AJS but retiring from the 500cc when the exhaust pipe of his Norton broke – and at Aberdare Park the following Saturday. There he won both 350 and 500cc finals but then had to dash away, missing the final invitation race, to catch a plane to Italy, where he was due to meet Count Agusta to finalise plans for Monza. The talks were successful, and in my race report in *MCN* I reported that 'on Sunday, at the Italian Grand Prix, Mike Hailwood wrote yet another page in his fabulous book of success. Having his first outings on the MVs he scorned the prophets who say it takes a year to learn to ride the Italian "fours" by winning the 500cc class after a fierce scrap with Gary Hocking which only ended when the World Champion [Hocking had already clinched the title] overdid things and slid off his MV with four laps to go.'

On that hot sunny day in Italy Mike made yet more motorcycle racing history by competing on three four-cylinder machines. His first outing was his début on an MV Agusta in the 350cc race, and he had already proved his mastery of the machine by clocking the fastest lap in practice, ahead of Hocking. Mike took the lead from the start but was then caught by Hocking, who went on to win. After finishing a close second Mike was out again in the next race – the 250cc. During practice McIntyre had been fastest ahead of Mike, and in *MCN* I wrote: 'The 250cc race was positively frightening! Five works Honda "fours" tore ahead from the flag – McIntyre, Redman, Phillis, Hartle and Hailwood. For lap after lap only inches separated them'. Inevitably the pace told. Hartle slid off, Phillis's machine slowed, and then McIntyre crashed heavily when an oil leak soaked his rear tyre. That left Redman and Hailwood to fight it out to the flag, where Jim got his nose ahead to win by a wheel. Mike had the twin consolations of a record lap at 114.06mph (183.52kph) and the knowledge that he had virtually clinched the World Championship. There to see the fun was Honda boss Soichiro Honda, attending his first-ever European race, and he must have marvelled at the sheer stamina of Mike, who was on the line for the 500cc race within minutes of being flagged home in the 250cc – the three main classes being run consecutively after the programme-opening 125cc race.

During practice Hocking had responded to the new Hailwood threat by breaking the absolute motorcycle record for Monza, lapping two seconds faster than Mike. The Welsh-born Rhodesian took the lead from the drop of the flag, but Mike soon caught him and they delighted the huge crowd by constantly swapping first place until Hocking crashed, leaving Mike – who had covered just over 300 racing miles (482.7km) on three different bikes in five hours – to win. All in all it had been an historic day – and not just for Mike. For after flying from Milan back to London, driving up to Kettering to the *MCN* office, completing my race report with results and finishing off the Paddock Gossip column, I finally staggered up my garden path at 3am to find that my wife Peta had given birth to our first child earlier that night. We resisted the temptation to call her Monza and plumped for Joanne instead!

Those three races had taken their toll. Mike pulled out of the next weekend's Cadwell Park meeting, the first on the new and much longer circuit and the first-ever international event on the Lincolnshire track, saying his wrists had not recovered from their Monza pounding. Obviously he preferred to get fit for the Swedish Grand Prix at the flat and rather featureless Kristianstad circuit. Redman had to win to keep his championship hopes alive, and when he took the lead and pulled away it looked as though they would both have to travel out to Argentina for the final round in October. However, they were spared the expense when Redman crashed, letting Mike through to win and

clinch his first world title at the age of 21. Earlier in the day the cheerful Czech Franta Stastny (Jawa) had outlasted the MV Agustas to win the 350cc race, Hocking retiring with ignition problems while Mike limped home seventh after missing gears and bending valves. They nevertheless got their act together for the final race of the day and gave a demonstration of team riding, with Hocking the eventual winner by a few yards from Mike, the pair of them lapping the entire field.

The 1961 season ended with the usual blur of British races, Mike competing in four in the space of two weeks. At the Mallory Park 'Race of the Year' he rode his Norton into second place behind Hocking on his MV Agusta and won the 350cc event on an AJS; at Aintree he won all four main events on Mondial, AJS, and Norton; at Oulton Park he won two out of three; and at the last meeting of the season, at Brands, he won the 250cc race Mondial-mounted but hit bike problems in both the bigger classes.

Was it time for a rest after a hard, successful season during which he had won his first World Championship, finished a challenging second in the 500cc, earned a fully-fledged works ride with MV Agusta, and again won the 500cc ACU Star? Not a bit of it. The week after Brands, Mike was competing in Spain on the tree-lined one-mile (1.61km) park circuit in Zaragoza. There he led the 125cc race on an ex-Ubbiali works MV Agusta until an oil leak developed and he slid off while leading. Nothing daunted, he turned out on a 500cc four-cylinder MV Agusta and won the main race by two laps. Then it was back to England and off to America for the second time that year, where he and South African Paddy Driver had been invited to compete in a race at the Willow Springs circuit in southern California in November. They decided to make a holiday of it, travelled across the Atlantic in the luxury liner *Queen Mary* with a van containing two 500cc Nortons, and then drove nearly 3,000 miles (4,827km) across the United States from New York to Willow Springs.

As their first World Championship winner, Mike had hoped that Honda would lend him a factory four for the 250cc class. However, despite this publicity opportunity in a booming bike market the factory and their

American minions completely ignored his presence. But because at that time the American Motorcycle Association was not a member of the FIM, and none of their riders were allowed to compete, the opposition was weak and Mike won with a record lap. Driver was suffering from food-poisoning and retired. When Mike finally reached home after a sojourn in Arizona (where the van broke down), he found he had been voted 'Man of the Year' by the readers of *MCN*, after being placed in the first three for the previous three years. He also came fourth in the BBC Sports Personality of the Year contest, which was won by Stirling Moss.

Mike later admitted that all this success rather went to his head. He moved out of the family home away from Stan's professional and steadying influence, and into a flat, and spent the winter enjoying wine, women, and song. When I interviewed him soon after I had switched from *MCN* to *Motor Cycling* early in 1962, and asked him about his plans, he replied: 'I haven't a clue. I live for the day and all I know is that I'll be racing for MV this year.' He said he did no fitness training but liked to relax by playing the clarinet and piano and going to jazz events. I described him then as an '11 stone, 5ft 11in genius on two wheels … already established as one of the greatest road racers our sport has ever seen.' A BP advertisement of the time claimed he had won 220 races during his four years of racing with them (1958–61 inclusive) and had broken 160 lap and race records during the same period.

Mike then flew out to the Bahamas to join Stan and step-mother Pat for a holiday, from which he broke off to ride a Norton in the second US Grand Prix at Daytona. There he led the race until the engine seized on lap 36 of the 40-lap event, letting Takahashi through to win on a works 250cc Honda. Even when he arrived home from that early February race in the States his plans for 1962 were far from clear. He had an agreement to race works MV Agustas in the World Championships and to ride other machines in British and Continental events, but there was no chance of him defending his 250cc crown on a Honda.

His first race in Europe was a 'warm up' meeting at Modena on 19 March. There he retired from the 250cc race when his MV Agusta twin suffered ignition trouble, but he led the 500cc class on the bigger MV Agusta from start to finish. Despite this win he came back from Italy a very disgruntled man and was surprisingly outspoken when I interviewed him, saying: 'I have never been so disorganised in my life. I could not get Count Agusta to agree to a race programme. His motto seems to be "if I can't win I won't race!"' Obviously not worried about the autocratic Count's reaction, Mike continued: 'I wish I had stayed with Honda – in fact I'd go back to them if they would have me. I've not the slightest idea when or where I will be having my next outing on an MV.' He also said he was disappointed not to have raced the 125cc MV and was afraid that the failure of the 250cc would mean that the Count would not allow him to race it again.

He made his first appearance on a British circuit that season at Mallory Park on 1 April, the day before his 22nd birthday. There he won the 250cc class on an ex-works Benelli single borrowed from Shrewsbury racer-dealer Fron Purslow. Then his AJS let him down in the 350cc class, stopping with ignition trouble, but he finished strongly with a win on his Norton in the 500cc race. The next week he announced that he hoped to race one of Joe Ehrlich's new water-cooled two-stroke singles in the 125cc classics, including the TT, and just days later he raced the EMC into second place at Silverstone, beaten by inches by similarly mounted Derek Minter.

A quick trip to Italy for the Imola Gold Cup meeting proved disappointing. The outdated Benelli single gave trouble, and two pit stops to clear blocked jets dropped Mike to fifth place in the 500cc race – hardly a result to impress Count Agusta. Neither was Mike impressed when the promised pair of MV Agustas failed to arrive in time for the Good Friday meeting at Brands Hatch. He finished third there on the little EMC and won the 350cc event on his AJS, but suffered problems with a six-speed gearbox he was trying in his 500cc Norton. However, the Italian fours arrived for Sunday's Snetterton meeting. There Mike scored a 350/500 double on his British début on the fours and repeated this success at Thruxton on the Monday.

Thruxton was followed by four Continental meetings: the non-championship Austrian Grand Prix held on an interesting little circuit that used the end section of the autobahn by Salzburg; the opening World Championship round in Spain; the French Grand Prix a week later; and another non-title race, the Grand Prix of the Saar. He won the 500cc race in Austria with a record lap but was surprisingly beaten in the 350cc by Stastny on a factory Jawa four-stroke twin. Both the Spanish and the French events catered for lightweights only – no 350 or 500cc races – and Mike's only rides were in the 125cc class on Ehrlich's EMC, in which he finished fourth in Barcelona but disappointingly slid off while challenging the Hondas in France. But things came right for Mike and EMC in the Saar. There he won the 125cc race with team-mates Rex Avery and Paddy Driver, making it a 1–2–3 for the British bikes. He retired from the 500cc race and then headed for the Isle of Man for his fifth week of TT racing. His first outing, in the 250cc event riding the Purslow Benelli, proved eventful. Outpaced by the leading Hondas he hung on to third place until slowed by a loose streamlining on the fourth lap. When he stopped at his pit the complete fairing was removed, and although he now had no chance of a place he sportingly continued, only to retire on the last lap with engine trouble.

His next race was the 125cc, in which he gave the Honda team a scare by holding second place for two laps only for the gearbox to fail on the third and final round. That afternoon he was out on the 350cc MV Agusta in a race which proved to be both tragic and dramatic. Mike and team-mate Gary Hocking, the reigning class World Champion, were both out to win and faced, for the first time, a challenge from Honda, who had moved up into the division with a 285cc version of their famous four, ridden in the TT by Phillis and McIntyre. Hocking took the lead from the start, pursued by Hailwood and the Hondas. Then on the second lap Phillis crashed at Laurel Bank and died on the way to hospital. McIntyre retired with a misfire a lap later, but there was no let-up for the leaders, with Hocking leading Mike into the last of the six laps by just nine seconds. Then, due to the hard-slogging and probable over-revving, both machines began to misfire, and Hailwood came home the winner by 5.8 seconds – the closest finish since 1950. His speed of 99.59mph (160.24kph) was a record and he had also set a record lap at 101.58mph (163.44kph).

Despite being deeply troubled by the death of Tom Phillis, Hocking rode brilliantly to win the 500cc Senior TT, while Mike was slowed by gearbox and clutch trouble and eventually limped home in 12th place after spending 13 minutes at his pit while his mechanic rebuilt the clutch. Both then travelled over to Mallory, where Mike finished second on the Benelli to Redman (Honda) in the 250cc race, won the 350cc on the smaller MV Agusta, and made it a double by beating Hocking by a split second in the 500cc event. The next day – Whit Monday, 11 June – Gary Hocking flew to Italy to discuss his future with Count Agusta while Mike raced the two MV Agustas at Brands Hatch, crashing and then remounting to finish fourth in the 350cc class and winning the 500cc. Then came the bombshell news that Hocking had decided to quit racing. He had seen too many good friends killed and the death of Phillis had been the final straw. After meeting Count Agusta he had flown on to his home in Bulawayo. Ironically he was killed racing a car later the same year.

Rumours that Mike was to get a new 250cc four-cylinder Benelli for the Dutch TT proved unfounded and his day started with a nasty shock when Redman, on the 285cc Honda, got the better of him in the 350cc race – in fact he had to ride hard to finish second ahead of the young Italian Silvio Grassetti on a Bianchi twin. Things looked good for Mike in the 125cc race when he shot ahead on his EMC from the start and quickly built up a lead, but then his engine tightened, forcing him to ease up; he eventually finished a close fifth. Only in the 500cc class did things go according to plan, Mike winning easily with the record lap in the bag.

Mike again suffered problems with the little EMC at the Belgian Grand Prix the next weekend. There the exhaust cracked and he finished fourth. With no bike for the 250cc race and no 350cc event in the programme his only other outing was in the 500cc class, which he won easily to take the lead in the World Championship. After the Belgian it was on to the lovely Solitude circuit in the forest outside Stuttgart for the German Grand Prix. Curiously, like the earlier Spanish and French rounds, this catered only for the lightweights, and with no 250cc this meant a single outing on the EMC for Mike. Fastest in practice, he was right up with the leading Hondas until slowed by an unusual problem – his helmet strap had come loose! He lost time adjusting it, dropping to sixth, but fought back to split the Hondas and finish third, behind Luigi Taveri and Tommy Robb but ahead of McIntyre.

Back in England Mike rode in three meetings in two weeks but did not win a single race. At Castle Combe he finished third on a misfiring AJS in the 350cc race, and second on his Norton to similarly mounted Minter in the 500cc final. At Snetterton the AJS seized and he came off the Norton, but at Oulton Park he did better with a second on the AJS and a third in the 500cc race on a Reg Dearden Norton. But this meeting too ended in tragedy, when McIntyre crashed while racing a Norton in the 500cc race. He died from his injuries a few days later, the second top flight rider to die in the space of just two months.

Mike suffered two disappointments when he crossed from Oulton Park to Dundrod for the Ulster Grand Prix the next weekend. To start with there was no EMC for him to race in the 125cc event, and then the 350cc MV Agusta developed terminal engine trouble when he was leading after having seemingly 'seen off' the new full-sized 340cc Hondas of Redman and Robb. There was no such opposition in the final race of the day – the 500cc. Mike won as he pleased, finishing over three minutes ahead of Alan Shepherd (Matchless) while at the same time raising the lap record to 99.99mph (160.88kph), despite the absence of anyone to push him.

The Ulster was followed by a mad dash across Europe to the Sachsenring for the East German Grand Prix – and there Mike sprang a real surprise. Tired of waiting for the half-promised Benelli four he asked MZ technical chief Walter Kaaden if he could race one of the East German-built MZ two-stroke twins in the 250cc class. Starved of racing because the politics of the time made it impossible for the East Germans to compete in NATO countries, Kaaden was delighted, and the outcome was a sensational race between Mike and Honda captain Redman. In my report in *Motor Cycling* I wrote: 'With never more than inches in it, the lap record was shattered time and again, and in a breath-taking climax that had the whole crowd [said to be 280,000] in a frenzy Redman tenaciously held on to win despite a fantastic

lap at 100.77mph [162.14kph] by Mike'. This lap was, in fact, faster than Redman's new 350cc record, set earlier in the day when he rode the new big Honda to a third classic success, easily beating Mike – on the bigger, heavier, and older MV Agusta – into second place. Completing 244 racing miles (392.6km) in a day, Mike then finished by winning the 500cc race in which, refusing to take it easy, he lopped over five seconds off Hocking's old lap record with a round at 104.50mph (168.14kph).

The Italian Grand Prix at Monza was something of an anti-climax. Mike retired early in the 125cc race when his EMC failed, crashed while riding an uncompetitive Benelli single in the 250cc event, and was a non-starter in the 350cc because Count Agusta was afraid he would be outclassed by the Hondas. However, he did win the 500cc race, virtually unopposed, to clinch his first 500cc World Championship. He was the youngest rider ever to win the title, a record which stood until 1983 when American Freddie Spencer (Honda) took the championship at the age of just 21.

There was an even bigger anti-climax at his final European race-outing of 1962, at the Finnish Grand Prix, held on a dangerous, tree-lined park circuit at Tampere. With MV Agusta not interested, Mike only went there to honour an agreement to race the works MZs in this non-NATO country. He crashed heavily when the 125cc model seized during practice and was lucky to get away with just a heavily bruised chest and torn leg muscles. However, these injuries prevented him riding in the end-of-season British events and provided a thought-provoking end to a mixed season. True, he had won the 500cc title, but without real opposition it had been a hollow victory and his efforts in the other classes had been frustrated by factory politics, unreliable machinery, and broken promises.

A proud moment as Mike sits on a works four-cylinder MV Agusta for the first time before going out to practise for the 1961 Italian Grand Prix at Monza. Left is MV Agusta race-manager Nello Pagani, right is Bill Webster (known as 'Websterini' because of his close links with the Italian factories), while the mechanic is Vittorio Carrano. (Mick Woollett)

Above left *Waiting for the start of the 125cc 1961 East German Grand Prix at the Sachsenring. Mike's Honda twin suffered plug trouble in the race, which was won by the man behind him, Ernst Degner (MZ).* (Roland Priess)

Above *A sea of spectators, part of a 150,000-strong crowd, crane forward to watch the start of the 500cc 1961 Dutch TT. Gary Hocking (MV Agusta, 1) won the race from Mike (Norton, 2). Others in the picture include Frank Perris (Norton, 24) and Bob McIntyre (Norton, 7), who finished third.* (Mick Woollett)

Left *Mike and his Bill Lacey Norton on their way to second place in the 500cc 1961 East German Grand Prix. Mike finished second to Gary Hocking and the works four-cylinder MV Agusta in five of the first six grands prix, successes which earned him a place in the Italian team.* (Wolfgang Gruber)

Right *Engines roar into life at the start of the 500cc 1961 Ulster Grand Prix with Mike (Norton, 30) masking winner Gary Hocking (MV Agusta, 45). Others prominent in this picture are John Hartle (1), Peter Middleton (26), Ray Spence (41), and Rob Fitton (22), all on Nortons.* (B.R. Nicholls)

Left *Tony Godfrey (Norton) leads Mike (AJS) by inches as they battle it out in the 350cc final at Aberdare Park in late August 1961. Mike won this race and the 500cc final as well before dashing off to fly to Italy for the Italian Grand Prix.* (B.R. Nicholls)

Above *On the rostrum after finishing second to winner Gary Hocking (right) in the 350cc 1961 Italian Grand Prix, Mike's first race on an MV Agusta. He was soon back on the podium, as winner of the 500cc race!* (Mick Woollett)

Right *Moto-cross star Jeff Smith (left) feels the Hailwood stubble as Tony Godfrey (second left) and the then-reigning 250cc moto-cross World Champion Dave Bickers look on. This picture was taken at the Winchester scramble in December 1961.* (B.R. Nicholls)

Left *At the BBC Sports Personality of the Year presentation ceremony in December 1961 winner Stirling Moss (right) and Mike, who finished fourth, discuss the 500cc Norton that carried the latter to second place in the World Championship.* (B.R. Nicholls)

Below *Jim Redman on a works four-cylinder Honda leads Mike on Fron Purslow's single-cylinder Benelli during the 250cc race at Silverstone early in 1962. Redman won, but they shared the fastest lap at 90.53mph (145.66kph).* (B.R. Nicholls)

Right *Close-quarters cornering at Brands Hatch in April 1962 as Mike (AJS) leads Phil Read (Norton) wearing an unfamiliar helmet. Mike went on to win.* (B.R. Nicholls)

Far right *This shot of Mike in winning action on the 350cc MV Agusta at Snetterton on Easter Sunday 1962 shows just how big the old-style four-cylinder was. This was his British début on a works MV Agusta.* (B.R. Nicholls)

Below right *Autobahn action as the field gets away at the start of the 500cc Austrian Grand Prix, 1 May 1962. The race was run on a circuit using a section of the autobahn near Salzburg. It was won by Mike (MV Agusta, 1) from Austrian Bertie Schneider (Norton, 4), with his compatriot Rudi Thalhammer (Norton, 3) – partly obscured by Hailwood – third.* (Wolfgang Gruber)

Right *Two winners – jovial Czech Frankie Stastny (left), who won the 350cc class on his Jawa twin, with 500cc winner Mike Hailwood at the Austrian Grand Prix on 1 May 1962. The bike is Mike's 500cc MV Agusta. (Wolfgang Gruber)*

Left *Face of a champion. This 'mug shot' of Mike was taken at the Austrian Grand Prix at Salzburg on 1 May 1962, when he was 22 years old and was the reigning 250cc World Champion. (Wolfgang Gruber)*

Below *Naked and unashamed! Mike started with a fairing on his Fron Purslow ex-works Benelli single in the 1962 250cc Lightweight TT, but when it started to break up he took it off at the pits and continued like this. Unfortunately engine trouble then put him out. (B.R. Nicholls)*

Below right *Sunshine and shadows as Jim Redman (Honda) leads Mike (EMC) over Ballaugh Bridge during the 1962 125cc Lightweight TT. Mike passed Jim and held second place in a race won by Switzerland's Luigi Taveri (Honda) until gearbox trouble put him out on the last lap. (Mick Woollett)*

Above *The 1962 350cc Junior was the closest TT for 12 years with Mike (MV Agusta, 3) beating team-mate Gary Hocking (MV Agusta, 6) by just 5.6 seconds after 226 miles (363.6km) of racing. This shot shows them accelerating out of Parliament Square, Ramsey.* (B.R. Nicholls)

Right *Anxious moment as Mike bumps the big MV Agusta into life at the start of the 1962 500cc Senior TT, with New Zealander Hugh Anderson (Norton) waiting his turn in the background. Transmission problems dropped Mike to 12th place in this race.* (B.R. Nicholls)

Left *Although the EMC was fast it was also fragile, but in the German Grand Prix at the Solitude circuit in July 1962 Mike, seen here leading Bob McIntyre (Honda) and Ernst Degner (Suzuki), kept going to finish third.* (Wolfgang Gruber)

Right *Having left Honda for MV Agusta, Mike elected to race a British EMC in the 125cc class during 1962. Here he prepares for practice at the Spanish Grand Prix in Barcelona in May while designer Joe Ehrlich warms up the bike. Mike led the race until the expansion chamber split.* (Mick Woollett)

Below *Mike's agreement with MV Agusta for the 1962 season left him free to race his own bikes on British circuits. Here, Norton-mounted, he leads eventual winner Derek Minter (Norton) at Oulton Park in August 1962.* (B.R. Nicholls)

Below right *A quarter of a million fans thrilled to this close finish of the 250cc race at the East German Grand Prix in August 1962, for Mike – seen here chasing winner Jim Redman (Honda) – was riding a locally-built, twin-cylinder MZ two-stroke.* (Mick Woollett)

CHAPTER 5

Doubts cleared up

The winter of 1962–3 proved to be one of rumour and counter-rumour, fuelled by indecision as Mike tried to resolve where his future lay. The only thing of which anyone was certain was that he was going out to South Africa again after a three-year absence, and that although this was intended mainly as a holiday he would nevertheless be racing a 350cc AJS and a 500cc Norton in a few events. After delaying his departure to take part in try-outs with car racing teams including Reg Parnell's, he flew out to Johannesburg to link up with his bikes, which had been shipped to Cape Town. Asked about his plans as he left Mike replied: 'When you hear them they will shock you!' And then, at his first South African meeting – at the Swartkops circuit near Pretoria in late November, where he won the 500cc class and finished second to Jim Redman on a Honda in the 350cc – a reporter claimed that Mike had said he was determined not to return to

Mike's three-fingered hand signal to photographer Nick Nicholls at Whitegates, Ramsey, indicates that his MV Agusta is only firing on three cylinders during the 1963 Junior TT. He certainly does not look downhearted about it, even though he later retired. (B.R. Nicholls)

MV Agusta for 1963. A week later, at Bulawayo, where he again won the big class but slumped to fourth in the 350cc behind Redman, Paddy Driver (Norton), and Bruce Beale (AJS), *Motor Cycling's* man-on-the-spot reported that Mike 'gave the impression he would very much like to join the Honda line-up as his car prospects are fading fast'. However, long-distance communication was difficult in those days, before the age of direct-dial telephoning, fax machines and e-mail, and the next report – from the end-of-year meeting at the East London circuit, overlooking the Indian Ocean – contradicted this statement and quoted him as saying: 'I'd not object to having another season on the Gallarate fire engines'.

That last meeting of his short South African season was disappointing. He retired from both races – with stone-shattered goggles in the 350cc and with a broken frame in the 500cc – and then flew home in mid-January. He was still confused about his future and told *Motor Cycling*: 'I can't tell you what I'll be doing this year ... I cannot make my mind up whether to race on four-wheels or two.' Denying rumours of a return to Honda as 'ridiculous' he confirmed that Count Agusta had made him an offer.

The whole scene changed dramatically when the Gilera factory announced that they were to return to racing after an interval of five years. Their bikes were to be the formidable four-cylinder racers on which Italian Libero Liberati had won the 500cc World Championship in 1957 and finished second in the 350cc class, while the team was to be managed by Gilera's three times 500cc World Champion, Geoff Duke. This put a whole new complexion on things. After five years of total MV Agusta supremacy there was to be real competition, and Mike's appetite was whetted. Spurred on by the Gilera comeback, Count Agusta invited Mike to fly to Italy with their mutual friend Bill Webster. At the Gallarate factory they agreed a contract which covered the 250, 350 and 500cc classes but which allowed him to race cars for the Reg Parnell team when not required by MV Agusta. The Count also agreed that Mike could race other bikes in British meetings, including his old Ducati twins that now belonged to John Surtees, provided his permission was sought and granted.

At last the doubts had been cleared up and Mike made his 1963 début at Modena on 19 March, where he won the 500cc race with ease, the Gilera team not being ready for such an early outing. Back in England for the season-opening Mallory Park meeting at the end of March, Mike reported that he had sold his AJS and Norton, which had just arrived back from South Africa, to Leighton Buzzard dealer Sid Mularney. With Sid's permission he rode the bikes, straight from the crate, at Mallory, but the AJS spluttered to a standstill with a blocked jet while the Norton carried him to second place behind Minter. However, he did score a win that day, on the Surtees Ducati in the 250cc class.

At Silverstone six days later the Ducati simply was not fast enough and the race was won by Redman (Honda), with Mike second. During the week tuner Bill Lacey had rebuilt the AJS and fitted a six-speed gearbox, and this proved a winning combination in the 350cc class. The 500cc race was historic, for it marked the first Gilera outing for five years. Unfortunately Mike had no MV Agusta for the race, finishing fourth on a Reg Dearden Norton, but he was not dismayed when Derek Minter and John Hartle made it a 1–2 for the Scuderia Duke Gileras, for neither got within a mile-an-

hour of the record lap of 100.51mph (161.72kph) which he had set on a Norton the previous year. After the race Mike said: 'The myth of Gilera invincibility has been well and truly exploded. I'm looking forward to Brands Hatch.' There, six days later, we were scheduled to witness the first MV Agusta versus Gilera clash of the new era at the Good Friday meeting.

The 500cc MV Agusta the Count had promised duly arrived, and so did a record crowd of around 60,000, but there was to be no 'clash of the giants' that day. For on the very last corner of the first race of the day Mike crashed while leading on his AJS. Although he escaped serious injury a sprained wrist made it impossible for him to operate the clutch of the big MV Agusta, and he had to sit and watch while Minter won the 500 and 1,000cc events. This time Minter did break the lap record, becoming the first to lap Brands at over 90mph (144.81kph) and proving that the Gilera challenge had to be taken seriously.

Mike made his comeback at Imola on 25 April and led the race until his weakened wrist gave trouble, eventually finishing third behind the two Gileras. After the race Mike paid a sporting tribute to winner Minter, saying: 'There is nothing in it for speed but the way Minter is riding at the minute I wouldn't attempt to stay with him – he's out of this world.' He then went to Salzburg for the non-championship Austrian Grand Prix. Because there was no lightweight for him to ride Count Agusta allowed him to race a 250cc MZ, but plug problems put him out after he had set a new lap record. With no Gileras present he won the big class unchallenged, again with a record lap.

Back home Mike went to spectate at Brands Hatch on 11 May, where Minter was racing a brace of Nortons. There, on the last lap of the last race of the day, a crash occurred that was to have a major effect on the season. Just a mile (1.61km) from the finish race-leader Minter went into a slide, and second-placed Dave Downer on Paul Dunstall's 650cc Norton 'Domiracer', too close to avoid the tangle of man and machine, crashed and was fatally injured. Minter escaped with back injuries which put him out of racing for three months and effectively put paid to Gilera's hopes for the season.

Lack of communication ruled Mike out of the first

classic, the German Grand Prix at Hockenheim. With no 500cc class Mike did not think that MV Agusta would send a bike for the 350cc race, so there was no one there to ride it when the MV Agusta mechanics arrived at the German circuit! In fact his next outing was the TT. This started with a disappointment when the promised 250cc twin MV Agusta failed to arrive, confining his activities to the 350 and 500cc classes. In the Junior race he simply could not match the pace of Redman on his Honda, but he did hold second place until the MV Agusta gave trouble on the fourth lap of the six-lap race. Speed trap figures for the 500s showed just how equally matched the two Italian fours were. Hailwood was fastest at 148.8mph (239.42kph), but Hartle on his Gilera was only fractionally slower at 148.3mph (238.61kph). In the race, though, it was Hailwood all the way with both race and lap records in the bag at 104.64mph (168.37kph) and 106.41mph (171.21kph) respectively. Hartle came second and Phil Read, who had replaced Minter on the second Gilera, third.

After the TT Mike went to Oulton Park, where he won his first car race driving his own Formula Junior Brabham, but he was soon back on bikes at the Dutch TT. At Assen he was easily beaten by Redman (Honda) in the programme-opening 350cc race. In the 500cc class Mike seemed to be in control when he shot ahead from the start and led the Gileras by 100 metres at the end of the first lap. But then the big MV Agusta 'lost' a cylinder, and after a pit-stop had failed to cure the problem Mike was forced to sit and watch a Gilera 1–2, with Hartle winning from Read, a result which put them first and second in the World Championship with 14 and 10 points to Mike's eight.

Eight days later it was a different story at the Belgian Grand Prix. In my report in *Motor Cycling*, I wrote: 'With a searing lap record at 125.61mph [202.11kph] Mike Hailwood showed exactly who is top dog when he thrashed the Gileras of the Scuderia Duke in the Belgian Grand Prix on Sunday.' With Hartle retiring and Read second it meant that Mike left Belgium as joint leader with Read in the 500cc table, both having scored 16 points. Minter was back for Mike's next race, the Ulster Grand Prix at Dundrod, where Gilera fielded a three-man team in opposition to Mike's lone MV Agusta. Early

in the day Mike had to give best to Redman on the Honda in the 350cc class but there was no doubt who the star was in the 500cc race. My race report in *Motor Cycling* stated that this was 'a magnificent victory for Mike Hailwood and MV! Laughing off a three-star Gilera challenge, MV's lone wolf scored yet another sensational win when he thrashed the entire Scuderia Duke in the 500cc class of Saturday's Ulster Grand Prix.' Mike won from Hartle and Minter by 42 seconds and, with race and lap records to his credit (at 99.27mph/159.73kph and 101.28mph/162.96kph), he took the lead in the championship with 24 points to Hartle's 20.

The next weekend Hailwood made history when he became the first rider ever to win three World Championship races at a single Grand Prix. This was at the East German meeting at the Sachsenring, and we headlined my race report in *Motor Cycling* 'A three-win Wonderman'. The event was split over two days that year, and Mike's first success came in the 350cc on the Saturday when he scored an unexpected win ahead of the previously all-conquering Hondas of Luigi Taveri and championship leader Redman. The second came in the 500cc when he again defeated the Gileras, his task made easier by the retirement of Hartle, who had a heart-stopping moment when his front mudguard broke and locked the front wheel. Mike completed his trio of wins by again trouncing the Hondas in the final race – the 250cc. Count Agusta had reluctantly agreed to Mike racing an East German MZ, just as he had the previous year when narrowly beaten by Redman (Honda), but he had been plagued by problems during practice and was back on the third row of the grid. Team-mate Alan Shepherd took the lead from the start, but Mike gradually caught him and then, to the delight of the massed spectators, went ahead to win, the MZ pair both finishing well ahead of Redman on the leading Honda.

This success was followed by a trip to Finland for the Grand Prix at Tampere. Mike showed his grit and determination in the 350cc race when, after being bumped off the track by the Russian Nikolai Sevostianov, riding a Jawa-style SKEB twin, he fought back to win. He then finished the day by winning the 500cc race to clinch the World Championship for a second year. Keeping his options open, Mike then raced in two events at Monza on successive weekends, first in the Formula 1 car grand prix, where he finished tenth driving a Lola-Climax V8 for Reg Parnell, and then in the motorcycle grand prix! He retired from the 350cc race with engine trouble but won the big event with a record lap at 119.99mph (193.06kph). Both the Gileras retired.

Mike's British season ended two weeks later with the 'Race of the Year' at Mallory Park. This saw the first clash on English soil of Mike on the MV Agusta and Minter on the Gilera, and I reported in *Motor Cycling* how 'Mike Hailwood and his fabulous MV set the seal on an incredibly successful season by thrashing the opposition in both wet and dry conditions to win the 500cc final and the £1,000 first prize Race of the Year.' Count Agusta then sent him off to win the final 500cc World Championship race in Argentina and rumours that he might quit bikes were finally scotched in mid-October when he revealed that, en route home from South America, he had called to see the Count and they had agreed a contract for 1964.

Mike's year should have ended at the Japanese Grand Prix in November, but when the Japanese organisers refused to pay expenses he took up the offer of a fun outing to the Moroccan Grand Prix at Casablanca. There he rode Tom Kirby bikes, winning on the 350cc AJS and finishing seventh on a 500cc Matchless after sliding off while disputing the lead with Paddy Driver.

A curious attack on Mike and Alan Shepherd by the FIM (the sport's international governing body) enlivened the winter months. Both were sent stern warnings by the FIM about misconduct at championship events and threatened with 'immediate suspension' if there were any further complaints. This was grist to the journalists' mill, and in *Motor Cycling* I commented: 'The whole thing is so preposterous, so feudal, that it is like something from a ridiculous dream.' Stan Hailwood instructed his solicitors to write to the FIM demanding clarification and specific instances of Mike's alleged misdemeanours. Eventually the whole thing fizzled out.

Mike's first outing on a bike in 1964 was at Daytona in early February. There he enjoyed a very busy Sunday, for in the morning he broke the classic one-hour record by covering 144.83 miles (233.03km) in 60 minutes on his normal road-racing MV Agusta; then in the after-

noon he won the 500cc class of the US Grand Prix, promoted to World Championship status that year. He was hard-pressed at Daytona by Benedicto Caldarella, a young Argentinean who had been lent a four-cylinder Gilera to promote sales in South America, and whose performance so impressed Gilera that he was invited to Europe, where he won first time out at Imola on 22 April, breaking race and lap records. However, Mike was not at that meeting. He had made his 1964 European début at Modena a month earlier, crashing and remounting to finish fifth, and had then won at Silverstone. His first clash with Caldarella since Daytona came at Cesenatico a week after Imola, where Mike won easily from Remo Venturi (Bianchi), with Caldarella coming third after a slow start.

Having cut his racing programme Mike's next outing was in the TT, where a bout of tonsillitis curtailed his practice sessions and forced him to scratch from the 350cc race. He also admitted to being 'wobbly and feeling a bit washed out' when he came to the line for the start of the 500cc Senior TT. But luckily there was no worthwhile opposition in the event, for Gilera were concentrating all their efforts on backing Caldarella in the Continental rounds of the World Championship. Hailwood won easily, but it was the slowest Senior since his Norton win three years previously.

At the Dutch TT Mike had a hectic time. First he practised in Holland, then flew down to Rouen to drive a Reg Parnell Lotus-BRM in practice for the French car Grand Prix, before flying back to Holland for the racing on Saturday. Here he was easily beaten by Redman (Honda) in the 350cc race but scored a comfortable win in the big class after Caldarella's expected challenge had first been hampered by a near crash and then eliminated by engine failure. Immediately after his win Mike jumped into his Jaguar to drive the 400 miles (643km) to Rouen to compete in the French Formula 1 car event, and then back to Spa-Francorchamps for the Belgian Grand Prix the next Sunday. Mike again won easily, and another victory in the German round at Solitude late in July confirmed him as the 500cc World Champion for the third year in succession at the age of just 24.

His task had been made easier by the absence of Caldarella, who had crashed and injured a foot in a non-title race at San Remo in Italy, but Mike was himself to suffer a race injury in his next meeting – the East German Grand Prix at the Sachsenring. With MV Agusta only providing a 500cc mount – on which he easily won the class – Mike had accepted the offer of a 250cc MZ and hoped to repeat his sensational win of the previous year. This looked to be on when he streaked ahead from the start and smashed the lap record with a round at 102.06mph (164.21kph), only to crash as he accelerated out of a slow corner. A gashed head, concussion, and torn shoulder ligaments stopped him from riding in the Ulster Grand Prix but he was fit for the Italian at Monza in mid-September.

However, he was a far from happy man. The problem was that Count Agusta refused to let him race the long-awaited, brand-new three-cylinder MV Agusta in the 350cc class. I reported at the time: 'I've seldom seen Mike so annoyed as he was at Monza.' The story was that the Count was afraid Mike would fall off the new bike and would be unable to race against a fully recovered Caldarella in the 500cc class. Although disgruntled, Mike duly won the big race with ease, and then had an MV Agusta flown over for his second and final outing of the English season, at Mallory Park on 27 September. As expected, he won both the 500cc event and the £1,000 first-prize 'Race of the Year' before turning his attention to a possible outing in the final World Championship race, the Japanese Grand Prix at Suzuka in November.

With no 500cc class and with the Count still unwilling to risk the new triple, Mike hatched a plan with Walter Kaaden to race a pair of MZ two-strokes, a 250 plus a slightly enlarged model in the 350cc class. And despite being offered only £70 starting money to cover the £1,000 expenses involved, Mike still went: 'For a bit of fun'. In fact the meeting was a farce, with just 24 competitors riding a total of 33 bikes in four classes. The 250cc suffered plug trouble, but on the bigger bike Mike gave Redman (Honda) a good race and finished second.

Later that year I interviewed Mike for *Motor Cycling* and asked if he would stay with MV Agusta for 1965. He replied: 'Frankly I don't know. If they make some more bikes I will but I'm sick of promises which are not fulfilled. And I'm also sick of having so few rides. This year I did not get enough to keep my eye in … conse-

quently when I turned out on the 250cc MZ in East Germany I was dead "rusty" – and when I tried to go fast I fell off.' Later in the interview he made a revealing comment when asked why he went car racing: 'I'm a lazy sort of person and frankly I'd rather be one of the boys in car racing than a top-liner in motorcycling. Trouble is that when you are the champion everyone expects the best and it's hard on the nerves trying to live up to it.' He confirmed he still did no special training and, asked if racing required any effort and had he modelled his style on anyone, he replied: 'No – on both counts. Luckily for me racing comes naturally.' Asked about favourite circuits he picked the Sachsenring in East Germany ahead of the TT 'because it has every type of bend, it's still a genuine road circuit, the organisers and spectators are tremendous and there's a terrific atmosphere.'

His successes and his trip to Japan had sparked off a wave of interest among the Far Eastern factories. Suzuki, Yamaha, and Honda were all eager to sign him for 1965 and for while it looked as though a deal was possible whereby Mike would race Suzukis in the smaller classes while continuing to ride for MV Agusta in the 350 and 500cc classes. This was favoured by Mike, who had slipped away for a holiday in the Bahamas, where Stan now lived in retirement. But Count Agusta had other ideas. He had decided to expand his racing programme, and in late January 1965 he summoned Mike to Italy. When I met Mike on his return he was smiling broadly and told me that he had signed a further 12-month contract and that the Count had promised him more races, including outings on the new three-cylinder 350cc. He also said the Count had enlarged the team by signing Morini's lightweight star Giacomo Agostini, who, like Mike, was the son of a millionaire father.

Keeping in trim riding a 250cc Greeves in local trials, Mike entered the US GP; but the race, on 21 March, proved just as farcical as the Japanese event of the previous November. He won the 500cc class by two laps and, angered by poor starting and prize-money, described the meeting as 'awful'. His first clash with Agostini came at Riccione in Italy at the end of the same month – and it was Agostini who won the 500cc race ahead of Mike, who suffered front brake problems.

However, he took his revenge two weeks later at Cervia where he easily beat his young team-mate.

Relationships with the Count soured when a bike promised for the Easter meetings at Brands Hatch and Snetterton failed to arrive and Mike was forced to borrow a 350cc AJS from Kirby and a 500cc Norton from Mularney. After a dreadful day at Brands he came back to win the 500cc event at Snetterton. He then jumped into a chartered plane and arrived at Imola in time for the major international race there the next day, Easter Monday. With no practice, he started the 500cc race from the back of the grid but came through to beat Agostini by six seconds. The first classic they contested was the German Grand Prix, back on the Nürburgring, at the end of April. Mike was unhappy when the Count decreed that Agostini would ride the 'three' on its world début in the 350cc class, leaving him on the old four-cylinder bike. Agostini covered himself in glory in the race by forcing Redman to ride so hard on his Honda that he crashed, and the MV Agustas finished 1–2. However, Mike won the big class from Agostini.

After an abortive outing at San Remo and a test session at Modena, Mike then crossed to the Isle of Man for the TT, where he at last made his début on the three-cylinder racer in the Junior event – only to have it break down on the fourth lap at Sarah's Cottage when he was leading by half-a-minute, thereby letting arch-rival Redman (Honda) through to win. The 500cc Senior TT turned out to be an epic – and Sarah's Cottage, halfway round the rain-sodden 37.7-mile (60.66km) circuit, again featured prominently, with both Agostini and later Hailwood sliding off their big MV Agustas here. Despite the fact that his bike was damaged Mike picked it up, literally kicked the handlebars straight, and rode on to a famous victory with shattered windscreen, bent clutch lever, and flattened exhaust megaphones. It was his third Senior TT win in succession and his seventh TT win in five years. Asked about the crash, he replied: 'I wasn't even going fast but one second I was aboard and the next I was sliding up the road on my backside. And when I picked myself up there was my mate Ago looking on'.

After a win at the post-TT Mallory meeting it was on to the Dutch TT, where Redman (Honda) got the better of him and the three-cylinder MV Agusta in the 350cc class, with Agostini third. Mike then won the 500cc class at record speed and with a record lap, and in Belgium – where there was no 350cc race – he again beat his Italian team-mate to win the big class. Mike made it six straight wins in the 500cc class at the East German round two weeks later – a success that confirmed him as the half-litre World Champion for a record breaking fourth year in succession. The 350cc race proved disappointing, when his 'three' suffered engine failure. It was 'same again' in the Czech Grand Prix at Brno, where the 350cc blew up and Mike won the 500cc class, finishing a minute ahead of Agostini.

Tired of hearing that he only won because he had the best bikes, Mike turned out on a mixed bag for the Hutchinson 100 at Silverstone in mid-August (missing the Ulster because there were no MV Agustas available) and confounded his critics by winning on all three. He rode a Kirby 350cc AJS, a BSA 650cc Lightning production machine and his MV Agusta in the 500cc. This prompted me to write in *Motor Cycling*: 'The MV makes Mike Hailwood myth was exploded once and for all at Saturday's Hutchinson 100 when, wet or fine, the four-times World Champion notched one of the most versatile hat-tricks of his sensational career.'

The Italian Grand Prix at Monza was next on the list, where Mike looked set to score his first win on the 350cc 'three' when he took the lead and pushed the lap record up to 117.68mph (189.35kph). Then rain swept across the track and he slid off. He escaped injury, and finished the day with an easy win in the 500cc race.

Mike finished his 1965 European campaign with outings at Mallory Park, where he won the 500cc race but slumped to fifth in the financially important 'Race of the Year' when he found the big MV Agusta hard to handle in the wet conditions; and at Brands Hatch in October, where he led the 350cc race until the clutch of his Kirby-AJS failed, won first time out on a 500cc Kirby-Matchless, and then slid off the same machine while leading the invitation event. Reporting the meeting, I wrote: 'Mike Hailwood was involved in three tremendous dices at the *Evening News* International Race of the South at Brands Hatch on Sunday and the World Champion came through with flying colours, really giving the 20,000-strong crowd their money's worth.'

Nervous moments before the start of Mike's first TT on the Clypse circuit, the 1958 125cc race, as tuner Bill Lacey cleans his goggles and Giuseppe Pattoni holds the Paton. Mike finished seventh. (Mick Woollett)

Just 18, Mike (right) lines up with established Italian superstars Tarquinio Provini (left) and Carlo Ubbiali after finishing third on his NSU Sportmax in the 1958 250cc Lightweight TT. Provini won the race from his MV Agusta team-mate Ubbiali. (Mick Woollett)

Above *Early Continental outing at the 1958 Swedish Grand Prix at Hedemora, with Mike on the right on his NSU number 5. He came through to finish second, beaten only by East German Horst Fugner (MZ), left. Both the works MV Agustas (Carlo Ubbiali, 2, and Tarquinio Provini, 3) retired.* (Mick Woollett)

Left *Mike won the £1,100 first-prize Mallory Park 'Race of the Year' five times. He is seen here on a four-cylinder 500cc MV Agusta at the 1963 event, with mechanic Vittorio Carrano.* (Mick Woollett)

Above right *Action from the 1964 Mallory Park 'Race of the Year' as Mike cranks the mighty four-cylinder 500cc MV Agusta round the Devil's Elbow.* (B.R. Nicholls)

Right *MV Agusta first raced their three-cylinder 350cc in 1965. This shot, from the Dutch TT, shows Mike heading for second place behind Honda's Jim Redman.* (Mick Woollett)

Above *Good Friday, 16 April 1965. Mike, nearest the camera, prepares to start on a borrowed 500cc Norton alongside Bill Ivy on Geoff Monty's Monard and John Cooper (Norton). Mike retired with bike problems but won on the same machine two days later at Snetterton.* (Mick Woollett)

Left *Just before the crash! Mike in action on a Tom Kirby 500cc Matchless at a sunny Brands Hatch in October 1965, just before he slid off.* (B.R. Nicholls)

Right *Mike raced the works five-cylinder 125cc Honda only once – in the 1966 Lightweight TT. Here he rounds Quarter Bridge on the little bike that revved to 22,000! He finished sixth.* (B.R. Nicholls)

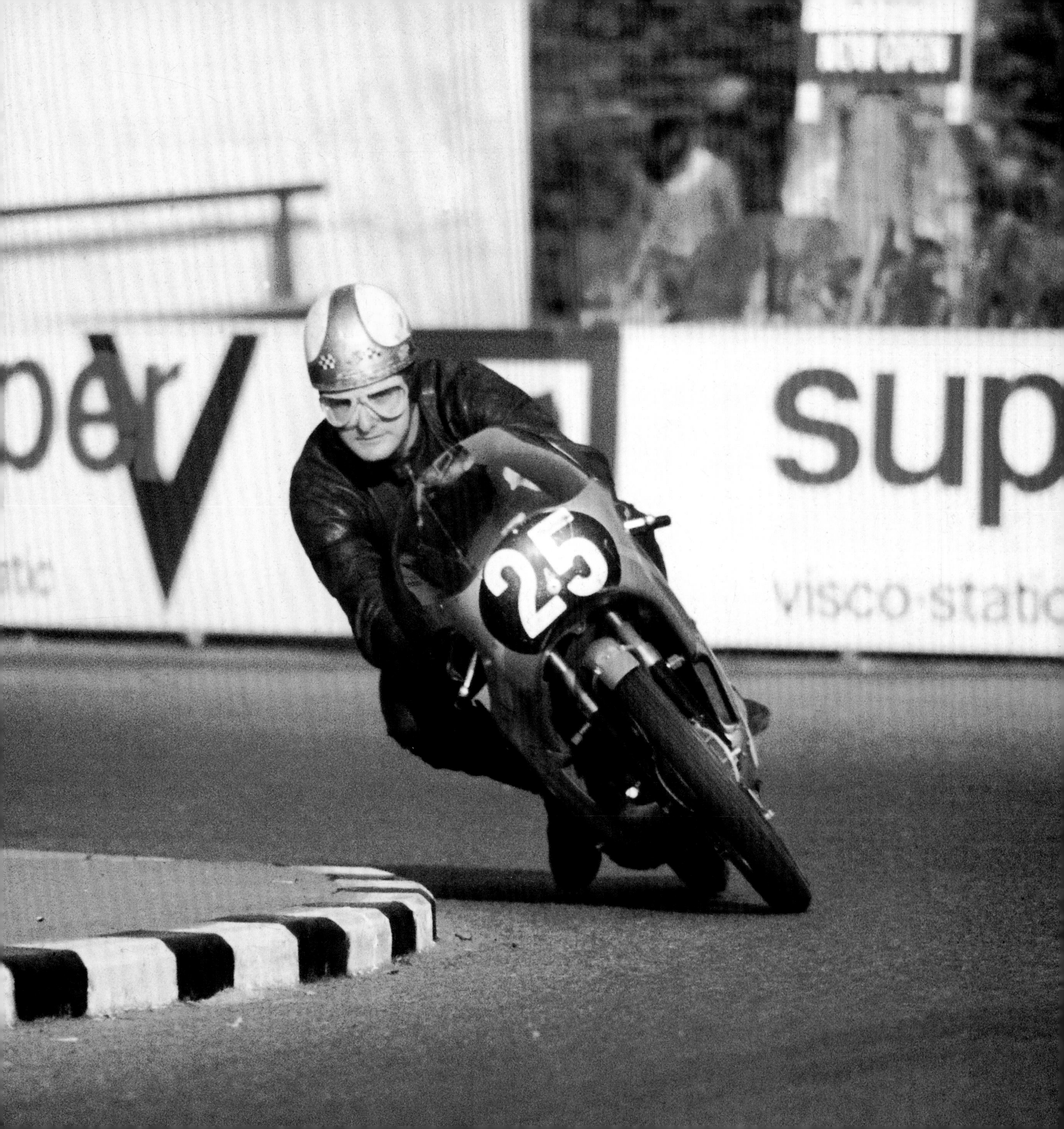
per
sup
visco-stati
25

Left *Rivals Mike Hailwood (left) and Phil Read at the June 1966 Mallory Park meeting, where Mike won the 350cc race on a Honda and Phil the 250cc on a Yamaha.* (B.R. Nicholls)

Right *Mike pushes the mighty four-cylinder 500cc Honda into life at the start of the epic 1967 Senior TT, during which he fought a titanic battle with Giacomo Agostini (MV Agusta). Mike set a lap record at 108.77mph (175.01kph) which remained unbeaten for a decade.* (B.R. Nicholls)

Below *On his way to another TT win, Mike sweeps his six-cylinder 297cc Honda round Whitegates Corner, Ramsey, in the 1967 350cc Junior TT.* (B.R. Nicholls)

Left *Sunshine, straw bales, and shadows as Mike (Honda) leads Renzo Pasolini (Benelli) and Bruno Spaggiari (Ducati) in the 350cc race at Cesenatico, Italy, early in 1968. Mike later crashed.* (Mick Woollett)

Above *Mike struggles with the bad-handling 500cc Honda during a sunny practice period at Cadwell Park in May 1968. It rained for the race and he could only finish fourth.* (B.R. Nicholls)

Above *Mike's only outing on a British circuit in 1969 was at Mallory Park in September, where he is pictured on one of the two 500cc Seeleys he rode that day – this one with the long exhaust megaphone. He finished third in the 1,000cc race and fifth in the feature 'Race of the Year'.* (B.R. Nicholls)

Left *Daytona 1971; Mike signs an autograph for a fan.* (Mick Woollett)

Right *Preparing for a pre-race team photograph – Mike astride his works three-cylinder 750cc BSA Rocket 3 at Daytona, 1971. He led the race until a valve broke. With him is American team-mate Jim Rice.* (Mick Woollett)

Left *Testing the 750cc Ducati at Silverstone in August 1971 – but Mike switched to a 350cc Yamaha for the racing. This was the Bologna factory's first 750cc, forerunner of the bikes raced so successfully by Carl Fogarty in the Superbike World Championships in the 1990s.* (Mick Woollett)

Right *Relaxing before his comeback ride in the 1978 Formula One TT, Mike (right) and Phil Read soak up the sunshine in the paddock. Mike won on a Ducati with Honda-mounted Phil second.* (Mick Woollett)

Below *Clutch start of the 1978 Formula One TT, and Mike (Ducati, 12) is just seconds away from starting in his first TT for 11 years. He won the race, with Ian Richards (Kawasaki, 11) third.* (Mick Woollett)

Above *Sunbathing spectators watch as Mike guns the big Ducati into Quarter Bridge during his winning ride in the 1978 Formula One TT.* (B.R. Nicholls)

Left *Action at Governors Bridge as Mike rounds the famous Isle of Man hairpin on a works 500cc four-cylinder Yamaha during the 1978 Senior TT.* (Mick Woollett)

Right *Mike scored the second win of his 1978 comeback campaign at Mallory Park, where he is seen on the Sports Motor Cycles' Ducati leading Phil Read (Honda) in the Formula One race.* (Mick Woollett)

Left *Preparing for the 1979 TT, Mike poses with the four-cylinder 500cc works Suzuki he later rode to victory in the Senior TT.* (Mick Woollett)

Right *Flat out at the Dutch TT in 1964. Here Mike is pictured on the bulky 350cc MV Agusta four-cylinder striving to close the gap on race-leader Jim Redman (Honda). The race was run in heatwave weather and was watched by a crowd of over 160,000.* (Wolfgang Gruber)

Below *Averaging a record 111.75mph (179.81kph) and with a record lap at 114.02mph (183.46kph), Mike screams his Texaco Heron Team Suzuki 500cc-four-cylinder racer into Ballacraine during his winning ride in the 1979 Senior TT. It was his 14th TT win.* (B.R. Nicholls)

Above left *Brands Hatch, Good Friday, April 1963, and Mike (AJS) leads Phil Read (Norton) out of Clearways. He crashed while leading and damaged a wrist.* (B.R. Nicholls)

Left *Mike at Silverstone early in 1963.* (B.R. Nicholls)

Far left *The chase is on. John Hartle (Gilera) leads Mike (MV Agusta) around Governors Bridge during the 1963 Senior TT, but Mike has made up most of the ten-second starting interval and went on to win, with Hartle coming second.* (Wolfgang Gruber)

Above *Two children peer through the railings at Signpost Corner as Mike screams by on the mighty 500cc MV Agusta to win the 1963 Senior TT.* (B.R. Nicholls)

Right *Ulster Grand Prix action, August 1963, with Mike (MV Agusta) leading Gilera-mounted John Hartle during his winning ride in the 500cc race.* (B.R. Nicholls)

Left *Smiling faces after the 500cc class of the 1963 Ulster Grand Prix, with winner Mike Hailwood flanked by runner-up John Hartle (right) and his Gilera team-mate Derek Minter.* (B.R. Nicholls)

Below left *One of Mike's most satisfying wins of 1963 came in the 250cc East German Grand Prix, where he beat class World Champion Jim Redman and his normally all-conquering Honda fair and square. Here Mike (MZ) leads Jim during that dice.* (Roland Priess)

Right *While at Daytona for the US GP in February 1964 the Hailwood equipe decided to try to break the classic one-hour motorcycle speed record. The bike was a normal four-cylinder 500cc MV Agusta racer, and here Charlie Rous – then with Motor Cycle News – checks the rear tyre while Stan Hailwood (right) has a quick smoke.* (B.R. Nicholls)

Below *Record breaking at Daytona Motor Speedway in February 1964. Stan gives Mike a signal and a thumbs up to indicate that he is on schedule to beat the old one-hour record of 141.37mph (227.46kph) set by Bob McIntyre on a 350cc Gilera in 1957. In fact Mike packed 144.833 miles (233.036km) into his hour.* (B.R. Nicholls)

Above left *After breaking the one-hour record, Mike competed in the United States Grand Prix in February 1964 and was surprised by the speed and skill of the unknown (to European fans) Argentine Benedicto Caldarella, who is pictured here on a works four-cylinder Gilera leading Mike in the 500cc race. Mike nevertheless came through to win.* (B.R. Nicholls)

Left *Forced to withdraw from the 1964 Junior TT because of illness, Mike had only a single ride in the Island that year, in the 500cc Senior. Though still far from fit he won the race, and is seen here on the big MV Agusta at Quarter Bridge.* (B.R. Nicholls)

Above *Mike cranks the MV Agusta into a fast left-hander during a winning ride in the 500cc 1964 Dutch TT.* (Wolfgang Gruber)

Right *A stern-looking Mike Hailwood mounts the rostrum at the 1964 Dutch TT after winning the 500cc race.* (Wolfgang Gruber)

Left *Massed crowds and the sweeping uphill curve above the Eau Rouge bridge form an impressive background as Mike aims for the apex of La Source Hairpin during his winning MV Agusta ride in the 1964 Belgian Grand Prix.* (Wolfgang Gruber)

Below *Mike guns the big MV Agusta to a win in the 500cc class of the German Grand Prix at Solitude in July 1964. It was a success that clinched the World Championship for a third year in succession.* (Wolfgang Gruber)

Right *Say cheese! Fixed grins from 'Race of the Year' winner Mike Hailwood (right), MV Agusta mechanic Vittorio Carrano and Honda's Jim Redman after another successful Mallory Park extravaganza in September 1964.* (B.R. Nicholls)

Below right *For the 1965 season Mike was joined by Giacomo Agostini on the works Agustas. Here he leads his young team-mate in the 500cc German Grand Prix at the Nürburgring. Beaten by Agostini in the 350cc race, Mike won this event with a record lap.* (Wolfgang Gruber)

Left *Mike Hailwood aged 25, pictured at the 1965 German Grand Prix at the Nürburgring.* (Wolfgang Gruber)

Right *Rain during the opening laps of the 1965 Senior TT made conditions treacherous. MV Agusta team-mate Giacomo Agostini crashed and so did Mike – but he remounted to win and this shot shows him completing the race on his 500cc MV Agusta despite a shattered windscreen, bent foot-rest, and flattened megaphones.* (B.R. Nicholls)

Below *Mike made his first appearance on the long-awaited three-cylinder MV Agusta in the 1965 Junior TT. Here he swings the Italian machine around Creg-ny-Baa with Kate's Cottage in the background. After setting a record lap at 102.85mph (165.49kph) and building up a 28-second lead he retired on the fourth lap with engine trouble.* (B.R. Nicholls)

Above *Trackside straw bales protect Wolfgang Gruber as he takes this superb shot of Jim Redman on a four-cylinder Honda being challenged by Mike on a three-cylinder MV Agusta during the 350cc class of the 1965 Dutch TT.* (Wolfgang Gruber)

Below *Weary but triumphant – Mike in the winner's enclosure after the 1965 Senior TT. With him (left to right) are MV Agusta team-manager Arturo Magni, Mike's father Stan, and mechanic Vittorio Carrano.* (B.R. Nicholls)

Above *Early stages of the 500cc 1965 Dutch TT with Giacomo Agostini (MV Agusta) leading Mike Hailwood (MV Agusta) just yards from the trackside spectators. Mike won the race.* (Wolfgang Gruber)

Below *That famous 'Mr Punch' chin is prominent as Mike urges his 500cc MV Agusta on to victory in the 1965 Dutch TT. Note how he has chamfered his boot away during cornering.* (Wolfgang Gruber)

Left *Paddy and Janet Driver's baby daughter looks anxious as Mike hams it up with the baby's bottle at the 1965 Dutch TT.* (Mick Woollett)

Right *Czech Grand Prix action as Mike hurls the big MV Agusta into a fast curve at over 100mph (161kph) on his way to winning the 500cc class at Brno in 1965. It was his seventh World Championship 500cc Grand Prix win in succession.* (Wolfgang Gruber)

Below *Mike obliges a young autograph hunter during a quiet moment at the 1965 Czech Grand Prix while team-mate Giacomo Agostini looks on.* (Wolfgang Gruber)

Left *Proving that he could win on equal bikes, Mike turned out on a 650cc BSA sports twin and beat all-comers in the production machine race at Silverstone in August 1965. Underlining this he also won the 350cc race on an AJS 7R, a model similar to that ridden by half the race entry.* (Mick Woollett)

Right *Typical short circuit 'scratching'. Mike on a Tom Kirby AJS leads the 350cc class at Brands Hatch in October 1965, with Dave Degens (AJS) nearly alongside, and Cyril Davey (Norton) and Peter Williams (AJS) close astern. Degens won the race while Mike slipped back to fifth with clutch trouble.* (B.R. Nicholls)

Below *Autumn sunshine lights up this 'happy snap' taken at Brands Hatch in October 1965. It shows (left to right) Mike, sponsor Tom Kirby (who provided the AJS and Matchless machines the three rode that day), Bill Ivy, and Paddy Driver. Mike led them to a 1–2–3 in the main event.* (B.R. Nicholls)

CHAPTER 6

Back to Honda

Well before the end of the 1965 season rumours began to circulate suggesting that Honda were determined to get Hailwood to race for them in 1966. In September *Motor Cycling* ran a front page story under the headline 'Honda bid for Mike Hailwood' which said: 'Honda plan to launch a full-scale racing attack in 1966 to regain the pre-eminent position they held a few years ago – and the man they are trying to get to lead their new-look team is Mike Hailwood'. This was followed in early October by definite news from Mike himself that he had agreed to a one-off ride on a six-cylinder Honda in the 250cc class of the Japanese Grand Prix at Suzuka later that month. But he warned that the problem of conflicting oil contracts still had to be solved (he was a Shell runner, but Honda were under contract to Castrol). This was resolved when the Japanese factory agreed to lend him a bike, as they had in order to get round a similar problem in 1961, and he went out to Japan with divided loyalties. He was to race an MV Agusta in the 350cc class in support of Giacomo

Cheery chappie. Mike at Oulton Park in April 1966. (B.R. Nicholls)

Agostini – who would win the World Championship if he won with Mike second – while in the 250cc he would be riding to win on a Honda.

Even as Mike flew out Count Agusta issued a statement to the Italian press saying that, whatever the English press reported, Hailwood would be racing for MV Agusta again in 1966. For a while it seemed he would be proved right, for Mike described the Honda team organisation as 'little better than a shambles' and the handling of the Honda 'six' as 'awful'. And that was after he had won the 250cc race with a record lap! He also won the 350cc for MV Agusta at record speed and with a record lap – his only win on this machine. But the championship slipped through Agostini's fingers when his bike spluttered to a standstill with a broken contact breaker spring when he was in the lead, Jim Redman (Honda) finishing second to take the title.

In November the contest to sign Mike was resolved in Honda's favour. *Motor Cycling* reported 'The clash of the giants is over. Honda have won the battle of the payroll from Count Domenico Agusta. Mike Hailwood signed to ride for the Japanese factory before leaving Tokyo for

South Africa with his ex-rival and new team-mate Jim Redman last week'. It then became clear why Honda had been so determined to sign Mike: they had decided to move up into the 500cc class and wanted the world's four-times 'heavyweight' champion on their bike. Good news for British enthusiasts followed when I reported in my Sport Gossip column in December that Mike was to have a 350cc four-cylinder Honda for use on the home circuits, although this was tempered by the fact that Honda would not allow him to race any other make of machine.

Honda launched their biggest roadster yet, the 450cc 'Black Bomber' twin, on the British market in February 1966 and initially there were plans for Mike and a co-rider to race one in the 500-mile (804.5km) sports machine race scheduled for Brands Hatch in June. However, this idea foundered because the CB450 had double overhead camshafts and the regulations did not allow this.

A tussle now went on behind the scenes as to who would race the 500cc Honda when it made its début at the German Grand Prix at Hockenheim in late May. Honda had wanted their six-times champion Redman to retire and concentrate on running the team, leaving the riding to Mike, but the Rhodesian was determined to add the 500cc title to his list of successes before quitting. This bickering became public knowledge, and in April I reported in *Motor Cycling*: 'Honda will make their début in 500cc road racing at the German Grand Prix at Hockenheim on Sunday, May 22, but Mike Hailwood does not know yet whether he will be racing the big Honda or whether the Japanese factory will let their team captain Jim Redman fulfil his ambition by allowing him to ride in the 500cc championship.'

After testing the new racer in Japan Mike flew home to confirm that it was an orthodox across-the-frame four-cylinder bike, and to race his 'hack' 350cc four in three British meetings over the Easter weekend. At Brands Hatch on Good Friday he won the 350cc class but got well 'blown off' in the 1,000cc event by Bill Ivy on a 500cc Matchless and Dave Degens on a 650 Dresda-Triton. At Snetterton on the Sunday he was caught out by a squall of rain and crashed, his mishap being 'copied' by seven following riders before the race

was stopped. Typically of Mike, he won on the hastily repaired bike the next day at Oulton Park.

He then crossed to the Continent for three lucrative early-season events before the serious business of the World Championships started in Spain. At Imola his year-old Honda proved no match for the latest Italian machines and he battled home third, beaten by Agostini (MV Agusta) and Tarquinio Provini (Benelli); at Cesenatico in Italy the next weekend Agostini retired, leaving Provini to win with Mike second; and at the Austrian Grand Prix on 1 May he won a poorly supported event. Then it was down to Barcelona for the Spanish, where the biggest class was the 250cc. It was the first time Mike and Jim Redman had clashed on Hondas since 1961, and it ended in victory for Mike and a fiery departure for Jim, whose Honda caught fire after he crashed.

In Germany the dispute over who should ride the new 500 was resolved in Redman's favour. Two of the big bikes had arrived in Germany, both had practised, and it looked as though things were swinging in Hailwood's favour when Redman's engine failed – at which point tactics as well as politics came into the reckoning. Honda wanted to win all three big classes, but the total race distance came to more than the 500km-per-day limit imposed by the FIM. This limited the riders to two races. The team therefore telephoned Japan for a ruling and it was decided that both should ride in the 250cc to counter the threat of Phil Read and Bill Ivy on the Yamahas; that Mike should race the 350cc against the very real threat of Agostini on the MV Agusta 'three'; leaving Redman to give the 500cc Honda its début against the lesser challenge of the Italian on the old MV Agusta 'four'.

The Honda tactics proved sound. Mike won the 250cc race from Redman with a record lap and made it a double by taking the 350cc honours too, again with a record lap, while Redman won the 500cc class from Agostini. The next week there were only three classes at the French Grand Prix at Clermont-Ferrand – 250cc, 350cc, and sidecars. Hailwood scored another double, easily beating Redman in the 250cc and finishing well ahead of Agostini in the larger capacity class, again with both lap records to his credit. This was followed by an overnight dash to compete on the 'hack' Honda at

Brands Hatch the next day, Whit Monday. Redman raced the bike in the 350cc event, finishing second to Read (Yamaha), while Mike rode it to victory in the major event, the 1,000cc.

With the TT postponed until the end of August because of a seamen's strike, his next outing was at Mallory Park in mid-June, where he won the 350cc race on the 1965 Honda ahead of Read (Yamaha). Then it was over to Holland for the second round in the Mike-versus-Jim 500cc saga, which was given added interest when Agostini arrived at Assen with a brand-new bike for the class – a 350cc 'three' with the capacity enlarged to 420cc. Mike started the day by easily beating Agostini in the 350cc race, run on a wet track, and he won again in the 250cc event, beating Read, on a four-cylinder Yamaha, into second place ahead of Redman.

In fact Mike was in such devastating form that most expected him to make it three wins in a day when the riders formed up for the 500cc race. But he had been plagued by problems during practice and had never ridden the bike on which he faced the starter. This had been built overnight using a 350cc frame and an engine rebuilt after a 'blow up'. It refused to start when the flag dropped and Mike was last away, cutting through the field to third place in a single lap and then, with a record lap, taking the lead on the fourth. Pulling away, he seemed to have the race won until his gearbox stuck in neutral going into a slow corner and he crashed. Agostini then pulled away in turn, to lead Redman by eight seconds at one stage before the Rhodesian put in a great ride to peg him back, take the lead, and eventually win by 2.2 seconds. This put him firmly in the lead in the 500cc table with 16 points to Agostini's 12, and left Mike without a single point. Hailwood was far from happy, and I wrote in *Motor Cycling* after the race: 'My spies inform me that the behind-the-scenes struggle in the Honda camp as to who shall win the 500cc World Championship rages just as strongly as it did in Germany where Jim Redman "commandeered" Mike Hailwood's Honda after his own had broken during practising'. I went on to say that a win in Holland would have resolved the matter in Mike's favour but that had not happened.

As far as Honda was concerned the whole business was resolved at the Belgian Grand Prix the next weekend. First Mike fought and won a tremendous battle with Read (Yamaha) to win the 250cc race at a record speed of 122.33mph (196.83kph) with Redman third. After a few minutes rest and a visit to the winner's rostrum, where he admitted that this had been his hardest race for a long time, Mike was straight out on to the grid for the 500cc race.

During practice the two Honda riders had seemingly established their superiority over Agostini, who had switched from the 420cc 'three' raced in Holland to one of the heavier and bulkier old 'fours' which were slightly faster and thought to be more suitable for the ultra-quick Spa-Francorchamps circuit. It was also during practice that the Honda mechanics worked out the top speed of their big fours as 169.24mph (272.31kph), causing Redman to quip: 'It won't do 170!' Allowing for wheelspin the true maximum was probably around 160mph (257.44kph), and it was Redman who had lapped the fastest at 126mph (202.73kph) – better than the lap record, one second quicker than Mike, and six ahead of Agostini. Hailwood had suffered problems with his gearbox, a recurring theme with the big Honda, and for the race got his mechanics to gear the bike up so that he only had to use the first five ratios in the 'box, thereby cutting out the troublesome top gear.

Then the weather, always unpredictable in the hilly Ardennes region where the circuit is situated, took a hand. Lightning streaked the sky as the field formed up on the grid and rain started to stair-rod down as the field got away. Agostini took an early lead but Hailwood soon passed him, only to be re-passed on the second lap. Redman completed the first lap in third place but the torrential rain was flooding the track and his big Honda aquaplaned as he approached the sweeping Stavelot corner on the far side of the circuit. He crashed at well over 100mph (161kph) and slid off the circuit, breaking a bone in his left forearm. Despite the conditions Mike fought back to regain the lead, but then gearbox trouble forced him out and Agostini toured round to complete the 15-lap, 131.41-mile (211.44km) race at just 98.91mph (159.15kph), some 24mph (38.6kph) slower than the 250s! This win put the young

Italian at the top of the 500cc table with 20 points while Mike still had to score.

While Redman flew home to South Africa in an attempt to get fit for the Ulster in August, Mike headed for East Germany and his favourite Sachsenring circuit. But after winning the 250cc race he was outpaced by Agostini on three-cylinder MV Agustas in both the 350 and 500cc classes. In fact Mike eventually retired from both, from the 350cc with piston-failure and from the big class with a broken crank. The one redeeming feature of the event, from Honda's point of view, was that Agostini did not add to his 500cc score, but crashed at 120mph (193kph) when unchallenged and only six miles (9.65km) from the end of the race, letting Franta Stastny (Jawa) through to win. Ago's MV Agusta was a shattered wreck after hitting a wall, and it was a very bruised and chastened young Italian who faced Hailwood seven days later at the Czech Grand Prix. Here, at the Brno circuit, Hailwood was in complete control. He won the 250cc race to clinch that World Championship, also won the 350cc, which put him into an almost unassailable lead in the class, and finished the day by cruising to a 500cc victory. It was the first time that anyone had ever won the three largest capacity classes at a World Championship Grand Prix in a single day, though Redman had beaten him to the trio by winning the 125, 250 and 350cc races at the Dutch TT in 1964.

Hailwood looked set to repeat this success at the Finnish round two weeks later at a new circuit at Imatra, right on the Russian border. He won both the 250 and 350cc races before fighting a high-speed battle with Agostini in the 500cc class. Then rain made the circuit slippery and Mike had to concede to the Italian after an excursion up a slip road. On his way to the Ulster Grand Prix, Mike rode in Bemsee's Hutchinson 100 meeting, run the 'wrong way round' at Brands Hatch. There he won the 350cc race on his old Honda but retired when leading on the same bike in the 500cc class when a gearbox oil-seal failed.

Mike could not race in all three classes at Ulster because of the distance-in-a-day limit imposed by the FIM. Having already won the 250cc title he naturally decided to give that a miss. He duly won the 350cc class

from Agostini to clinch his first World Championship in the class, and finished the day by again beating the Italian to win the 500cc race. Jim Redman had also flown in for the Ulster, but realised after a single lap of the Dundrod circuit that he was not fit enough to race. A week later he announced his retirement from international grand prix racing, a disappointing end to a glittering career.

Riders and bikes next went straight over to the Isle of Man for the postponed TT races, where Mike spoke to me about the Hondas, saying: 'The Honda six is a wonderful little bike to ride after the bigger ones. You can just screw it all on. I reckon it is easier to do a lap at 104mph [167.34kph] on the 250 than to get round on the 500 at 103 [165.73kph] – the big one is a real handful'. Despite the fact that he had broken race and lap records, he dismissed his victory in the 250cc TT, saying: 'I was nowhere near the limit … if I had gone any slower I'd have toppled over.' On the Wednesday of race-week he had two rides – in the 125cc TT in the morning, in which he finished sixth on his one and only outing on a five-cylinder Honda, and in the even more disappointing rain-delayed 350cc race, from which he retired with a broken valve after only a few miles.

On the 500cc Honda he had clocked 151.30mph (243.44kph) through the *Motor Cycling* speed-trap at the Highlander, the first rider to break the 150mph (241.35kph) barrier, but the bike was not handling well and Mike faced the race with apprehension, knowing that he had to win to keep his championship hopes alive. In the race itself on the Friday he led all the way, broke the lap record with a round at 107.07mph (172.28kph), won his ninth TT and his fifth Senior to beat John Surtees's record, and gave Honda their first Senior TT win. Yet when interviewed after the race he was not a happy man. I reported for *Motor Cycling* that 'pale and tired, he looked more like a beaten rider than a winner. He said he had had a million hairy slides and that the Honda was not handling at all well.'

Agostini, whose three-cylinder MV Agusta sported a full-sized 500cc engine for the first time, finished second and the two rivals went to Monza for the Italian Grand Prix with the title still undecided. There Mike won the 250cc race with a record lap, but despite having made the fastest 500cc practice lap he could not match the speed of the MV Agusta and retired when his over-stressed engine failed leaving Agostini to take the title he had won four years in succession.

Hailwood's racing year ended with two disastrous outings in England; at the Mallory Park 'Race of the Year' meeting where his 250cc Honda 'six' suffered a puncture when he was leading Agostini on his 500cc MV Agusta, and at Brands Hatch. He was a non-starter in the 350cc race at the latter, and then the crankshaft of his 250cc 'six' broke as he accelerated away from the start of the feature race. The Press and the crowd were far from happy, and *Motor Cycling*, headlining the story 'One Bike Mike Fails his Fans', reported: 'Mike's showing was pathetic … an appalling let-down for the fans'.

Honda then gave the Japanese Grand Prix, the final championship round, a miss, claiming that the new Fisco circuit was dangerous, and Mike flew out to South Africa to compete in a series of sports car races in a Ford GT40 lent to him by Bernard White, winning the three-hour Dickie Dale memorial event teamed with David Hobbs. From there he wrote to *Motor Cycling* to say he was fed up with the abuse he had received following the Brands Hatch debacle and put his own side of the story.

Early in 1967 there was talk of a car versus bike contest over a single lap of the TT circuit, with Surtees on four-wheels and Mike on two, both using Honda power. This came to nothing and the first real news of Mike that year was that he had signed a contract with the Grovewood circuit-owning group who controlled Brands Hatch, Mallory Park, Oulton Park, and Snetterton, to race at ten of their meetings that year. To make sure he would be properly equipped, Mike had got a promise from Honda that they would supply him with a 250cc 'six' and a new 350cc 'four' for the home meetings, while he employed Honda race-mechanic Nobby Clark to look after them.

This plan got off to a false start when he had to withdraw from the season-opening Good Friday meeting at Brands Hatch because Honda had ordered him to fly to Japan to test his 1967 bikes. But he flew back for the Sunday meeting at Mallory only to be 'hopelessly outpaced'. In fact he was nearly lapped on his old 350cc

Honda and it was later found that there was no oil in one rear suspension unit. Typically he bounced back to win both 250cc and 350cc races at Oulton Park the next day, Easter Monday, despite crashing and remounting in the smaller capacity race.

Hit by a financial crisis, caused in part by heavy investment in their Formula One race programme, Honda had meanwhile decided to cut right back on motorcycle racing. They withdrew completely from the 50 and 125cc classes and expected Hailwood to win the three main solo divisions assisted by Ulsterman Ralph Bryans. To help Mike they had developed an enlarged version of the 250cc 'six' for the 350cc class. This had an actual capacity of 297cc. They also agreed to him trying various European-built frames in an effort to sort out the handling of the 500cc Honda.

His first Continental outing was at Cesenatico in April, where he won the 250cc event but retired from the 500cc with ignition trouble when well behind Agostini. Imola, scheduled for the next weekend, was cancelled because of a freak snowstorm, so his next outing was in the first World Championship round in Spain, where there was no 350 or 500cc race. Mike shot ahead from the start of the 250cc event, built up a half-minute lead, and then retired with a puncture, leaving Read to win on a greatly improved Yamaha four. Said Mike: 'That's the second time in seven months that a puncture has stopped me when leading. It cost me a thousand guineas [£1,100] at Mallory Park and now this.'

Despite agreeing to Mike experimenting with frames, Honda ordered him to revert to a factory-built frame for the World Championship races. To soften the blow a third new frame was flown to Hockenheim for the German Grand Prix, where Mike was due to race in all three classes. His first outing ended in disappointment when his 250cc Honda refused to run cleanly on all half-dozen cylinders and he had to retire after just two laps. He then went trackside to successfully encourage team-mate Bryans to win the race ahead of Read. In the 350cc race, which saw the début of the 297cc Honda 'six', Mike cracked the lap record and easily beat Agostini, but the day ended in yet another disaster when the crankshaft of the big Honda broke when he was half-a-minute ahead of the Italian.

The next weekend Mike again raced in three classes at Rimini on Italy's Adriatic coast, winning the 250cc, being beaten by Renzo Pasolini (Benelli) in the 350cc, in which he raced a 1966 'four', and finishing the day by winning the big class using a lightweight Colin Lyster frame. Rimini was followed by a drive across Italy and France to the 'lightweights only' French Grand Prix at Clermont-Ferrand – and another disappointment. For in the 250cc race Mike broke the lap record and built up a big lead over the Yamahas of Read and Bill Ivy only to be slowed by gearbox trouble which dropped him to third place.

On his way to the TT Mike competed at the Brands Hatch Whit Monday meeting, and we left the circuit thinking he had won all three of the races he had competed in – the 250cc, the 500cc on the Lyster-Honda, and the 750cc in which he again rode the 250cc 'six'. But he was later excluded from the 750cc race because it was limited to engines over 250cc as well as under 750cc!

During practice for the TT he had a narrow escape when he was passenger in Bill Ivy's Ferrari when they crashed at high speed in the Greeba area, the Italian sports car being seriously damaged when it hit a stone wall. After surviving the crash with no more than bruises this turned out to be Mike's most successful TT week since 1961. On the Monday he scored his tenth TT win on his 250cc 'six' to equal Stanley Woods' record set in the 1930s. Then he beat the same record by storming to yet another win in the 350cc race, during which he not only broke the class lap record but the 500cc absolute record too with a lap at 107.73mph (173.34kph). And to cap the week he won the 500cc

Senior TT on Friday – but only after a truly epic battle with Agostini on the MV Agusta 'three', which most who saw it reckon to have been the best TT race ever. During practice both riders had clocked over 150mph (241.35kph) through the speed-trap – Hailwood registering 154.8mph (249.07kph) and Agostini 152.5mph (245.37kph).

The Italian set the early pace, breaking the lap record from a standing start at 108.38mph (174.38kph), so that after two laps he led by 8.6 seconds. Hailwood then responded with a record lap at 108.77mph (175.01kph), but a 44-second pit-stop, during which he attempted to fix a loose twist-grip, dropped him to 11.6 seconds behind after four laps. On the fifth he steadily pegged Agostini back and took the lead, for the first time, at Ramsey, two-thirds of the way round the 37.7-mile (60.66km) lap. The huge crowd was held spellbound as reports of the two superstars' progress came over the public address system. Agostini regained the lead on the climb over the Mountain and was two seconds ahead at the Bungalow – only to have his chain break at Windy Corner, a devastating blow to the Italian, who was celebrating his 25th birthday that very day. This left Mike to finish alone to win his third TT of the week (all at record speeds and with record laps) and his 12th in seven years. Immediately after the race he said that he had been hampered by the loose twist-grip, which the work during his pit-stop had failed to fix, and that he thought that Agostini would have won if he had kept going.

It is a measure of his skill that the lap record Mike Hailwood set that day remained unbeaten by a 500cc machine for no less than nine years.

Racing as it used to be! A cobbled road and spectators just feet away as Mike heads for a 350cc win on a Honda at the 1966 Austrian Grand Prix, held over the old autobahn circuit near Salzburg. (Wolfgang Gruber)

Crash, bang, wallop at Snetterton on a wet Easter Sunday in April 1966. The first frame of this three-shot sequence shows Mike sliding gracefully down the track hotly pursued by his 350cc four-cylinder Honda as Dave Degens (Aermacchi) passes by. In the second picture Mike is on his feet as Bill Ivy (Kirby AJS) motors on. Then in the third frame two more join the mêlée. That's Lewis Young doing the acrobatics after dropping his AJS while Willy McClean (Norton) attempts to avoid the tangle and Mike (right) tries to pick up his Honda. In all, eight riders crashed before the race was stopped. (B.R. Nicholls)

Right Coming and going. Two pictures illustrating the dice between Honda team-mates Jim Redman and Mike Hailwood in the 250cc class of the 1966 German Grand Prix at Hockenheim. Jim leads Mike into the corner … and then out of it. Both are riding six-cylinder machines and Mike won the race with a record lap. (Wolfgang Gruber)

Above left *Start of the 350cc class of the 1966 Dutch TT, and Mike makes a trademark lightning getaway on his four-cylinder Honda. Chasing him are Derek Woodman (MZ), Giacomo Agostini (MV Agusta, 4), Renzo Pasolini (Aermacchi, 29), and John Cooper (Norton, 14).* (Wolfgang Gruber)

Left *Honda conference at the 1966 Belgian Grand Prix as Mike sits astride the immaculate but bad-handling four-cylinder 500cc Honda. He led the race until gearbox trouble put him out.* (Wolfgang Gruber)

Above *Another flashing departure as Mike screams his six-cylinder Honda into the lead at the start of the 1966 250cc East German Grand Prix at the Sachsenring. Chasing him is Heinz Rosner (MZ), with the white-streamlined Yamahas of Mike Duff and Phil Read prominent in the background.* (Wolfgang Gruber)

Right *Only 26, but Mike's hair is already receding as this picture taken at the 1966 East German Grand Prix proves! Behind Mike is Honda team-manager and top technician Michihiko Aika.* (Wolfgang Gruber)

Above *Mike hurries to a win in the 350cc class of the 1966 Czech Grand Prix riding a four-cylinder Honda. It was a memorable day, for he won the 250 and 500cc races as well. It was the first time anyone had won the three biggest classes at a World Championship event in a single day.* (Wolfgang Gruber)

Left *Slippery going as Mike navigates his 500cc Honda on a wet track to score his third win in a day at the 1966 Czech Grand Prix. It was Mike's first win on the big Honda.* (Wolfgang Gruber)

Right *Four leads six as Phil Read on his four-cylinder two-stroke Yamaha leads Mike on his Honda 'six' during the 1966 250cc Czech Grand Prix. Mike won the race.* (Wolfgang Gruber)

Far left *Keeping his 500cc World Championship hopes alive, Mike rounds the hairpin in the lead during the 1966 Ulster Grand Prix at Dundrod. He went on to win this race but eventually lost the title to Giacomo Agostini (MV Agusta).* (B.R. Nicholls)

Left *The Honda team at the 1966 Isle of Man TT, postponed that year from June to August/September because of a seamen's strike. Left to right: Mike, Jim Redman (who had just announced his retirement), Luigi Taveri, Ralph Bryans,* and Stuart Graham. The bike is Mike's race-winning 250cc six-cylinder. (B.R. Nicholls)

Below left *Ramsey Hairpin, 28 August 1966, and Mike is well on his way to another TT win, this time the 250cc Lightweight on his six-cylinder Honda. During the race he pushed the lap record up to 104.29mph (167.8kph).* (B.R. Nicholls)

Below *Cadwell Park in September 1966. Mike has made another good start and leads the 250cc field from Phil Read (Yamaha, 61) and Rod Gould (Bultaco).* (B.R. Nicholls)

Far left *Relaxing at his flat in Heston, west London, in 1966 – just taking it easy.* (Mick Woollett)

Left *Rare shot of Mike working on a motorcycle! Taken at Brands Hatch in March 1967, it shows Mike tightening a sparking plug while mechanic Nobby Clark holds the 350cc four-cylinder Honda. They were carrying out tests on the Colin Lyster double-disc front brake.* (Mick Woollett)

Below left *Perfectly poised and with his right foot skimming the track, Mike leads the 250cc 1967 Spanish Grand Prix at Barcelona. But a puncture in the rear tyre of his six-cylinder Honda cost him the race.* (Mick Woollett)

Below *This candid shot of Mike was taken at the 1967 German Grand Prix at Hockenheim. With him, deep in thought, is Honda race-chief Michihiko Aika, stopwatch in hand.* (Mick Woollett)

Right *After retiring from the 250cc 1967 German Grand Prix at Hockenheim Mike holds out a signal board urging team-mate Ralph Bryans to over-rev his six-cylinder Honda in an attempt to stay ahead of Yamaha rival Phil Read. It worked. Bryans won the race, a success that proved crucial to the destination of the World Championship.* (Mick Woollett)

Left *Dicing it out in the 250cc class of the 1967 French Grand Prix at Clermont-Ferrand. Winner Bill Ivy (Yamaha) leads from team-mate Phil Read and Mike, who was slowed by gearbox trouble.* (Mick Woollett)

Below *Mike makes it look easy as he heels his six-cylinder 250cc Honda around a left-hander during the 1967 French Grand Prix at Clermont-Ferrand.* (Mick Woollett)

Above left *Straining every sinew, Mike on his 500cc Honda chases Giacomo Agostini (MV Agusta) in the 1967 Senior TT. The picture was taken at Whitegates on the outskirts of Ramsey.* (Mick Woollett)

Far left *On his one and only ride in the Isle of Man on a 297cc six-cylinder Honda, Mike sweeps round the bend at Ginger Hall on his way to winning the 1967 350cc Junior TT. Mike loved this bike and set a new lap record at 107.73mph (173.34kph), which was faster than the existing 500cc record!* (Wolfgang Gruber)

Left *Dramatic moment in the 1967 Senior TT as rivals Mike Hailwood (Honda, nearest camera) and Giacomo Agostini (MV Agusta) pit-stop together. Mike eventually won the race, but only after the Italian's chain broke on the penultimate lap when there was only seconds in it.* (Mick Woollett)

Above *Urged on by the waving crowd at Creg-ny-Baa, Mike heads for victory in the 1967 Senior TT knowing that his rival Agostini is out of the race.* (Wolfgang Gruber)

Right *Stanley Woods, winner of ten TTs in pre-war days, congratulates Mike on beating his record by bringing his tally of TT successes to a round dozen during the 1967 race week.* (Mick Woollett)

CHAPTER 7

Others ride – Mike flies

The three Isle of Man TT victories in 1967 were not Mike's only trio of TT wins that year, for later the same month he blasted the opposition to dominate the Dutch TT, prompting a Continental enthusiast to comment: 'The others are riding but Mike is flying'.

Before crossing to Holland Mike and Agostini had clashed again in the Mallory Park post-TT meeting, where Mike won the 250cc class but retired from the feature race when his big Honda developed valve trouble. Agostini, already well ahead, went on to win. In Holland, Hailwood's day opened with an easy win in the 350cc class, the new 297cc Honda 'six' again proving superior to Agostini's three-cylinder MV Agusta. In fact Ago had to fight hard to stay ahead of compatriot Pasolini on a four-cylinder Benelli. Mike followed this up with another clear-cut success in the 250cc event, in which he finished half a minute ahead of Bill Ivy

Me and my shadow. Giacomo Agostini (MV Agusta) leads Mike (Honda) in the 1967 500cc Dutch TT, watched by a massive crowd. Mike, with a record lap, came through to win, his third victory of a day in which he covered 273 racing miles (439.26km). (Wolfgang Gruber)

(Yamaha). Only in the 500cc race did he face real competition. Agostini led for the first nine laps of the 20-lap event, but Mike was always in his slipstream and then took over to win with the absolute lap record in the bag. It was the second time he had won three classic races in a day and the fifth time he had scored a treble success at a World Championship meeting.

That it was Hailwood's sublime riding ability that was winning races for Honda was amply demonstrated the very next weekend at the Belgian Grand Prix. For on the old, ultra-fast 8.8-mile (14.16km) circuit his Hondas could not match the speed of either Bill Ivy (Yamaha) in the 250cc class nor Agostini (MV Agusta) in the 500cc. Reporting for *Motor Cycling*, I wrote: 'It was double disaster day for Mike Hailwood and Honda at Sunday's Belgian Grand Prix. In both the 250 and 500cc class his works Honda machines were so outpaced that not even Mike's brilliant riding could redress the balance'. The sheer speed of the improved four-cylinder 250cc Yamaha two-strokes was graphically illustrated when Phil Read shot into the lead and then lapped at 125.61mph (202.11kph) to shatter not only the class lap record but the 500cc one as well! And although the pace proved too hot for his engine, team-mate Ivy took over to win well ahead of the pursuing Hailwood.

With no 350cc class in Belgium Mike finished his day on the 500cc and the story was similar, with Agostini streaking ahead from the start to win by over a minute. Said Hailwood after the race: 'I don't know what MV have done to the bike but I just did not see which way it went today'. The Italian factory had certainly found some extra speed, for Agostini had pushed the lap record up to 128.58mph (206.89kph) – a record for a World Championship race. This success meant that Agostini and Hailwood now shared the championship lead with 22 points apiece, and Honda responded to the challenge by flying over a brand-new 500 for the next round, the East German Grand Prix at the Sachsenring. This had a lighter engine with magnesium crankcase and a stronger, stiffer frame. But the team's confidence in the new bike was undermined when it refused to start and it was found that the ignition timing was 180 degrees out!

Working through the night, the mechanics had the big Honda ready for the race, but Mike could not match Agostini and the MV Agusta and had to retire with gearbox trouble. The Italian won, with a record lap to his credit, and took the lead in the championship table with 30 points to Mike's 22. And this was Hailwood's second defeat of the day, for in the 250cc race he had been forced to retire when his engine failed while he was dicing for the lead with Read (Yamaha), a win which put the Yamaha rider ahead in that championship. Only in the day's opening race, the 350cc, had Mike finished first, his 297cc Honda again outpacing Agostini's MV Agusta.

A week later Mike hit back to win two out of three at the Czech Grand Prix at Brno. His first success came in the 350cc race, in which he scored his fifth straight win to clinch his second World Championship in the class and his eighth overall. Then came another defeat in the 250cc event, in which he took third place, beaten by over a minute by the duelling Yamahas of Read and Ivy. However, he finished the day a happy man, for a week's work had transformed the new 500cc Honda. Despite problems with a bent gearchange pedal he set a new lap record and held off the challenge of Agostini to win and

thereby keep his championship hopes alive. Though this success cut Agostini's lead to just six points (36 to 30), the gap opened to a massive 14 points when Hailwood crashed in spectacular style while pursuing Agostini in the rain-drenched Finnish Grand Prix at Imatra. The big Honda hurtled off the track and was badly damaged when it hit a tree, but Mike skidded to a halt unhurt. Within minutes he was out again for the 250cc race. This time the wet track was in his favour and he beat the Yamahas fair-and-square after a string of three defeats. This put him back in the title chase with 38 points to Read's 42 and Ivy's 40.

The next classic was the Ulster at Dundrod, but the organisers claimed Mike had not entered and threatened to bar both him and team-mate Ralph Bryans from the meeting. Said race organiser Billy McMaster: 'We are sick and tired of the way in which Mike Hailwood has messed us about. We have confirmed entries from all the other works teams and are able to use their names in publicity but all we've had from Mike, who is handling the Honda entries, is a series of cables from various parts of the Continent. We still do not know if he and Bryans are coming or not ... if we don't get confirmation by Saturday both will be out of the race.' Although never the most organised man when it came to paperwork, Mike responded in time, and on his way to Belfast raced in the Hutchinson 100 meeting at Brands Hatch, where he scored four morale-boosting wins.

Having already won the 350cc title Mike gave that class a miss in Ulster, preferring to concentrate on the 250 and 500cc. As in Finland, the big class came first and Mike made a superb start, tearing away and winning as he pleased with a record lap at 106.71mph (171.7kph). Agostini, on the other hand, was never in the hunt. He made an appalling start and was then slowed by clutch trouble which allowed Mike to close the championship gap – 38 points to the Italian's 44. The 250cc race quickly developed into a Hailwood versus Read duel, but on lap two the Yamaha rider left his braking a split-second too late, locked the front wheel, and slid off just feet ahead of the Honda. For an instant it looked as though Mike must hit the sliding bike and rider but he managed to squeeze through and away to win from team-mate Bryans, with Ivy, slowed by a misfire, coming in third.

This win leapfrogged Hailwood to the top of the 250cc championship table and he was now in with a very real chance of winning three titles in a year. Before crossing to Italy for the grand prix there in early September, Mike rode in two English events, at Snetterton and Oulton Park, scoring wins at both on his 250cc Honda. There was nevertheless a minor rumpus at Snetterton when, after being forced to pull out of the 350cc race when his old four-cylinder Honda failed, he was ruled out of the feature 'Race of Aces' event because his 250cc was too small! There was no such problem at Oulton, where he had entered only on the 250.

The Italian championship round proved disastrous. In the 250cc race the Yamahas were flying but Mike and team-mate Bryans hung on to them until Mike's engine blew on the third lap, forcing him into the pits with his bike covered in oil. Bryans then pushed the Yamahas all the way, but in a desperate finish it was Read who was first across the line, followed by Ivy and the little Ulsterman, with less than a second covering the three of them. That put Read back at the top of the 250cc table with 50 points, with Ivy and Hailwood joint second with 46 points apiece. This setback was followed by an even more galling defeat in the 500cc race when the gearbox of the big Honda began to fail while he was holding a seemingly winning lead over Agostini. With just four of the 35 laps to go he passed the pits waving his foot to indicate problems and the partisan crowd went wild as their hero gradually caught and eventually passed him with just over a lap to go. It was a success that virtually clinched the title for Agostini because he could now afford to finish behind Mike in the remaining round in Canada and still take the title.

Before flying out to Canada for the 'one off' World Championship race at Ontario's Mosport Park, sanctioned by the FIM as part of the country's centenary celebrations, Mike enjoyed a clean-sweep of six wins at two English circuits. First he won all three main races at Cadwell Park, and then, a week later, he repeated this performance at Mallory Park, where he also broke three lap records!

In Canada he won both the 250 and 500cc classes, but

his joy at keeping his quarter-litre championship hopes alive was tempered by the fact that Agostini took second place in the big class to clinch the 500cc World Championship for a second year. The two rivals, due to race at Brands Hatch the very next day, then shared a helicopter from the circuit to Toronto airport to catch the overnight flight to London. At Brands they clashed only in the 350cc race, which Mike won with a record lap. Then Agostini crashed in the 500cc event and the damage sustained by man and machine eliminated them from the feature 'Race of the South', leaving Hailwood to win easily on a 297cc Honda 'six'.

Mike's gruelling season, and the battle for the 250cc title, ended at the Japanese Grand Prix at Fuji in mid-October – and exactly who had won the World Championship was not cleared up until a week after the race was run. Both Hailwood and Read started the event with 50 points from their seven best placings in the 12 races held so far, but no-one seemed certain whether a tie on points would be decided in favour of the rider with the most wins or whether an extra race would be taken into account. The race itself turned out to be a complete anti-climax. At first Hailwood looked the favourite to clinch the crown when he took the lead, only to retire with ignition problems on the fifth lap. Then Read's Yamaha quit too, and the earlier hypothetical argument about who was the new champion became a real one. The FIM steward in charge of the meeting, Otto Sensburg of Germany, refused to rule. He claimed that the English and French FIM rule-books differed and left it to the FIM headquarters in Geneva to sort it out. From there Secretary-General Major Goode ruled that Read was the champion because in his opinion the 'one more race' rule came into operation.

By that time *Motor Cycling* had merged with *Motor Cycle* and I was sports editor of the new joint publication. We duly reported the outcome in our race report issue under the headline: 'Read tops in title tangle'. A week later we had to change our tune and report that, in fact, Hailwood had held onto the 250cc title. What had happened was that the FIM had changed the rules so that from 1965 championship ties would be decided in favour of the rider with the most wins, but this had not been included in the English version of the regulations. When it was applied Hailwood took the crown with five wins to Read's four.

Mike also won the 350cc race in Japan, with a record lap, and late in 1967 he was voted 'Sportsman of the Year' by the Sports Writers' Association as the man who, in their opinion had, 'contributed most to Great Britain's sporting prestige during the year'. However, doubts about his racing future became public knowledge when he said that he was not prepared to sign for Honda again until he had tested their 1968 machines. Bitterly disappointed at losing the 500cc title to Agostini and MV Agusta for a second year, he wanted to make certain the bikes for the new season would be competitive. It was also reported that he was having talks with Count Domenico Agusta about a possible return to the Italian factory team, but by this time he was again in South Africa, where he planned to race a 250cc 'six' and a Ford GT40 car. In fact he only rode in two bike events that season. At Pietermaritzburg on Boxing Day he won the 250cc race and the Dickie Dale trophy for the fastest average speed of the day, while at the Killarney circuit in Cape Town early in January 1968 he beat Jim Redman, making a comeback outing on an ex-works Yamaha twin, to win the 250cc race.

In between the two events he heard that his sporting achievements had been recognised in the Queen's New Years honours list with the award of an MBE. At first there was some confusion about the legality of this, because he had, a month earlier, reportedly become a South African citizen and given up his British nationality, saying he preferred the way of life out there and intended to live there when he retired from racing 'in three years'. Later, however, the award was confirmed, because Mike held a British passport at the time it was made and had not renounced his British citizenship in writing – and was not likely to. By mid-February there was still no definite news of his plans for 1968, and I wrote in *Motor Cycle*: 'What are Honda up to? That's the question that is puzzling the racing world.' Reporting that both Mike and Ralph had been summoned to Japan, I ended the item by saying: 'I've an idea that it'll be something that will curtail their racing activities. We should know by next week.'

Sure enough we did. Mike returned with the shatter-

ing news that Honda had decided to quit grand prix racing and would not contest the World Championships in 1968. This blow was then compounded, because he had signed a new contract with Honda which not only restricted him to racing the existing machines in meaningless non-championship events but also forbade him to ride any other make of machine.

Honda had taken this restrictive action for purely commercial reasons. They did not want 'their' World Champion joining a rival factory. The pity of it is that Mike fell for the bait of a big pay-off and the chance to make money at the lucrative non-championship events rather than quitting Honda and joining another team. To have done that would have cost him a lot of money for Suzuki too had pulled out of racing, Yamaha had Read and Ivy and did not need another star, and no factory in Europe could afford the sort of money needed to counter the Honda offer. In any case, the prospect of a carefree season without the pressure of the World Championships must have been enormously appealing after ten hard years in the top flight. Honda made available a 297cc 'six' for the 350cc class and the still hard-to-handle 500cc four-cylinder with its unreliable gearbox. Mike had to provide transport and mechanics but had total freedom as to when and where he raced, provided it was not a championship event.

During the winter Ken Sprayson of Reynolds Tubes had built Mike a new frame for the big machine, and he used this in the season-opening meeting at Rimini on 24 March. With Brands Hatch closed for repairs Mike had no chance to try the bike before setting out for Italy, but things looked promising when he stormed ahead from the start and broke the lap record. He then slid off but still remounted to finish second. Earlier in the day he had beaten Agostini on his MV Agusta 'three' to win the 350cc race, but on his second outing on the 'six', at Cesenatico two weeks later, he crashed and retired. It was his first defeat in the class since the 297cc machine had made its début at the German Grand Prix almost a year previously.

Mike was still experimenting with the 500. At Cesenatico he tried a Rickman front fork and a Lockheed disc front brake under the supervision of moto-cross star Derek Rickman. These did not prove to be the answer, for he was well beaten by Agostini, though a wet track did little to aid the experiment. Mike switched back to the original Honda fork and massive drum brake for Imola a week later, and on a dry track he beat Agostini and his World Championship-winning MV Agusta with surprising ease. In the smaller class he again retired after a crash, which meant that he had fallen off in all three of the early Italian meetings. So much for a quiet life!

The Italian meetings ended at Cervia in mid-April, where Mike again lost out in the 350cc class, in which, hampered by brake-fade on the punishing stop-go circuit, he could only finish third behind Agostini and Renzo Pasolini (Benelli). But he again won on the Reynolds-framed Honda. Then, after a flying visit to South Africa, he returned to England to race at Cadwell Park on 19 May – his only confirmed entry in a British meeting so far that year because the circuit-owning group which controlled Brands Hatch, Oulton Park, Mallory Park, and Snetterton had introduced a 'no start money' policy, which did not appeal to Mike. This played into Cadwell's hands. Circuit owner Charlie Wilkinson had no such inhibitions, signed Mike up, and then sat back when a record 40,000 fans beat a path to the Lincolnshire circuit to see their hero in action. He duly won on the 297cc with a record lap but once again found the bigger machine impossible to race on a wet circuit and struggled home in fourth place in the feature race.

Interestingly, commercial sporting events on Sundays were still not legal in England at that time, but legislation to allow paying-gate events on the Sabbath were being debated in parliament in June when Mike crossed to the Isle of Man for the TT. His Honda contract did not allow him to race on the island, but he said he preferred to spectate there rather than accept the offer of a race in Canada. Canada's loss was our gain at *Motor Cycle*, because we quickly agreed a deal for Mike to write an exclusive TT column for us with me as the link-man.

He started his first report by saying that he had been offered bikes by Count Agusta for the 1969 season and was considering his future: 'It's the terrific strain of responsibility that has robbed racing of most of its plea-

sure for me during the past couple of years. You go to a meeting knowing everyone from your bosses down to the youngest spectator is expecting you to win.' He continued revealingly: 'Take last year. Honda insisted on me doing three TTs – 250, 350 and 500cc. This meant I was out practising in nearly every session, stumbling about at 4.30am for the early morning ones and hardly ever getting a decent night's sleep. The smaller bikes were reasonable but the big'un was a real shocker. It nearly drove me round the bend. It simply would not steer even in a straight line. I suppose it was capable of over 160mph [257.44kph] but every time I was working it up towards its maximum it would hit a ripple in the road and that would start it going. It would begin to weave all over the place just as though it had a hinge in the middle … I cannot begin to describe the antics that bike got up to.' He went on to say: 'I haven't heard a word from Honda since I went to Japan early in February. And even if they were to return to racing, which seems unlikely, I don't think that I could stand any more.'

After his holiday in the Isle of Man, Mike returned to race in the post-TT Mallory Park meeting, where racing was delayed for an hour by a strike of riders protesting because the circuit-owning group, faced by the success of the Cadwell meeting, had changed their tune and were paying start money to the stars. The lesser lights felt this was at the expense of reduced prize-money. When racing did get under way Mike won two races on his 297cc 'six' – the 350cc and the main event for bikes up to 1,000cc, in which he beat TT winner Agostini on his 500cc MV Agusta.

He then took another break, but while on holiday in Switzerland with his former Honda team-mate Luigi Taveri he was persuaded to ride in a hill climb. It was at Monte Generoso near Lugano, up a six-mile (9.65km) minor mountain road, and he finished up with a broken collarbone after crashing a borrowed 250cc Honda 'six'. The accident occurred where the road crossed a railway track. Asked for his comments, Mike replied: 'That's my first and last hill climb. Imagine a thousand or so Governors Bridge hairpins end-to-end and a road no wider than a single track. The railway crossing had a ramp over it for practising but they forgot it on race day!' He made his comeback at the Hutchinson 100 at Brands Hatch in mid-August. Despairing of ever getting the big Honda to handle, he had arranged to race a single-cylinder Seeley if the big class was restricted to near 500cc machines. In the event it was not and he won the three main races on his 297cc Honda.

Just before he flew out for another South African holiday he told me he had been offered works MV Agustas for the Italian Grand Prix at Monza in September. At first he hesitated, but after either clearing or, perhaps, choosing to ignore the Honda contract problem he accepted the Count's offer. When he returned he rode in two English meetings before he left for Italy. At Snetterton on August Bank Holiday Sunday he won the three major races, including the 500cc on the Reynolds-framed Honda. The next day at Oulton Park he surprised and delighted the crowd by winning the 500cc class on a Seeley. His decision to race the British single was prompted by the wet conditions but he again proved he could beat all-comers on equal machinery.

In Italy things got political. Mike started by practising on a pair of three-cylinder MV Agustas but pulled out of the deal when Count Agusta insisted that he should finish second to Agostini in both races. He was happy to agree to team orders for the smaller class but not for the 500cc. He then switched to a 500cc Benelli last raced by Pasolini in the previous year's TT, but in a wet race crashed on braking while chasing Agostini. His 1968 season ended with outings at Mallory Park, where he won the big-money 'Race of the Year' for the fifth time and the 350cc race, both on his 297cc Honda; at Riccione, where he came third despite gearbox problems on the 500cc Benelli; and at Brands Hatch in October, where he won the two main events on his 297cc Honda.

Describing newspaper stories that he had decided to retire as 'rubbish', Mike flew out to South Africa for the 1968–9 season and sent his smaller Honda and an Iso Grifo car by sea. On arriving he moved into a new house built for him near Durban, and then rode in a single race at Pietermaritzburg on Boxing Day, winning with a record lap. He then competed at Killarney near Cape Town, winning the main event with a lap record amid more retirement rumours. These were seemingly confirmed in the 29 January 1969 issue of *Motor Cycle*, when, under a banner headline 'Hailwood Quits', we reported: 'The blow feared by millions of motorcycle racing enthusiasts has fallen. Mike Hailwood, probably the greatest road racer of all time, has quit the sport.'

Weary of bike racing and determined to race cars, where the pressure to win was far less, Mike had finally decided to make the break – but it was not as simple as that. In March the organisers of the Riccione meeting in Italy offered him four million lire (about £2,660 at that time – enough to buy a new Ferrari!) to ride the 500cc Honda at their meeting at the end of the month. It was the largest appearance money offer in the history of the sport. Commenting 'It's an awful lot of money. I'd be a fool to turn it down,' Mike accepted, prompting the apt headline: 'Mike snatches one-race bait'. Predictably he was well beaten by Agostini on his MV Agusta, but he did finish second.

He missed spectating at the TT and after a car-racing excursion to New Zealand, Chris Lowe – chief negotiator for the circuit-owning Grovewood group – persuaded Mike to ride in the Mallory Park 'Race of the Year' meeting in late September. With no Hondas available for this event, he borrowed a 500cc Seeley and put on a worthwhile show for a man who had not raced for nearly six months. He won his heat in the supporting 1,000cc class, finished third in the final won by Agostini on his factory MV Agusta, and then came fifth in the £1,100 first prize main event, beaten only by Agostini and riders on larger capacity twins.

Due to Honda's race policy and the poor state of the sport in general it was the end of two years in motorcycle racing limbo for Mike, who was still only aged 28. But it was by no means the end of the story.

Honda calculated the top speed of the 500cc Honda as close to 170mph (273.5kph) on the big gear it pulled at the 1967 Belgian Grand Prix – but here Mike brakes to little more than walking pace for the acute La Source hairpin. (Mick Woollett)

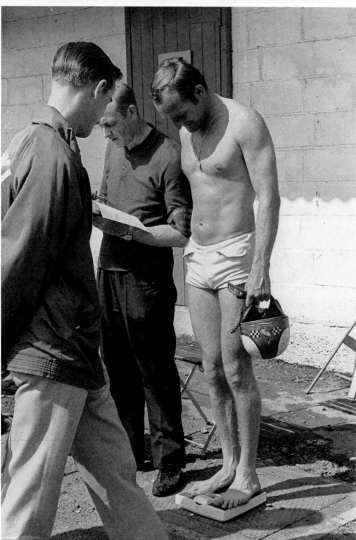

Above *More action from the 1967 500cc Dutch TT as Giacomo Agostini (MV Agusta) leads Mike on the big Honda round the tight de Strubben corner.* (Mick Woollett)

Left *Former team-mate Stuart Graham walks by as Mike weighs in at the 1967 Belgian Grand Prix – a formality for the multi World Champion, who was well over the FIM's minimum for riders.* (Wolfgang Gruber)

Right *Unprotected Armco barrier lines the Belgian Grand Prix circuit in 1967 as Mike, on his six-cylinder 250cc Honda, tries to close the gap on race-leader Bill Ivy (Yamaha). But the Japanese two-stroke proved just too fast and Mike had to be content with second place.* (Mick Woollett)

Below *Realising he has no chance of catching Giacomo Agostini and his flying MV Agusta in the 1967 500cc Belgian Grand Prix, Mike grimaces at the author. During the race Agostini put in a record lap at 128.58mph (206.89kph).* (Mick Woollett)

Above *Phil Read (Yamaha) matches Mike's flying start in the 250cc class of the 1967 East German Grand Prix at the Sachsenring. Chasing them is Ralph Bryans (Honda, 105), Heinz Rosner (MZ, 101), Derek Woodman (MZ, 103), and Bill Ivy (Yamaha, 114). The leaders fought a great battle until Mike retired, leaving Read to win from Ivy and Bryans.* (Wolfgang Gruber)

Left *A sea of spectators faces Mike as he guns his 297cc six-cylinder Honda around the uphill final bend of the 350cc class of the 1967 East German Grand Prix. Crowds of a quarter of a million were normal at the Sachsenring.* (Mick Woollett)

Right *Battle-weary after another hard day's racing – Mike Hailwood after competing in three races at the 1967 East German Grand Prix.* (Mick Woollett)

Left *It's a serious business! No smiling faces as Mike (right) and Giacomo Agostini stand on the rostrum at the 1967 East German Grand Prix after the 350cc race.* (Mick Woollett)

Below *Roadside spectators get a good view of Giacomo Agostini (MV Agusta) leading Mike (Honda) in the 350cc class of the 1967 Czech Grand Prix. Mike won the race with a record lap to clinch the class World Championship for a second year.* (Wolfgang Gruber)

Right *Real road racing. In 1967 half the grands prix were run on genuine road circuits. Here Mike (Honda) leads Giacomo Agostini (MV Agusta) through a village during the 500cc Czech Grand Prix. Note spectators on the roof. Mike won the race.* (Wolfgang Gruber)

Below right *The 250cc class of the 1967 Ulster Grand Prix – Mike (Honda) avoids the tumbling Phil Read (Yamaha), who crashed braking for the hairpin. The second picture shows Mike accelerating away to win the race and to take the lead in the World Championship.* (Mick Woollett)

Above *Time for a quiet chat! Mike (right) and Giacomo Agostini (MV Agusta) on the line at the Mallory Park 'Race of the Year' meeting in September 1967, where Mike won all three major races.* (B.R. Nicholls)

Left *Spring in Italy can be cold. Mike tries to keep warm by wrapping a tent around himself at Rimini in March 1968. It was his first race after Honda announced they had quit the grands prix but would allow him to race in lesser events.* (Mick Woollett)

Right *Rimini, March 1968, and Mike – his Honda fitted with a British-built Reynolds frame – leads Giacomo Agostini (MV Agusta) in the 500cc class. But Ago soon passed him to win.* (Mick Woollett)

Far left *Four of the best in action in the 350cc race at Cesenatico in April, 1968, with Mike (Honda) leading Giacomo Agostini (MV Agusta), Renzo Pasolini (Benelli), and Phil Read (Yamaha). Mike slid off and Pasolini won the race.* (Mick Woollett)

Left *Flares were all the rage when this picture of Mike was taken at Oulton Park in September 1968, on the Seeley he borrowed to win the 500cc race.* (Mick Woollett)

Below left *Proving yet again that he did not need a special bike to win, Mike (Seeley) leads the 500cc race at Oulton Park in September 1968 from Phil Read (Matchless) and John Cooper (Seeley).* (Mick Woollett)

Right *A pensive looking Mike Hailwood deep in thought at the 1968 Italian Grand Prix, where plans for him to race works MV Agustas fell through when Count Agusta insisted he must not try to beat Agostini.* (Wolfgang Gruber)

Below *Having turned down the offer of works MV Agustas, Mike raced a Benelli in the 500cc class of the 1968 Italian Grand Prix at Monza. Here he is seen at speed on the Italian four-cylinder machine before a crash put him out.* (Wolfgang Gruber)

Above *In late September 1968 Mike won the Mallory Park 'Race of the Year' for the fifth and final time. The picture shows him (nearest camera) getting away on his 297cc six-cylinder Honda while Giacomo Agostini is already flat on the tank of his MV Agusta.* (B.R. Nicholls)

Left *Mike's only outing on a British track in 1969 was at Mallory Park in September, where he rode a Seeley in the 'Race of the Year' meeting. Here he talks to Colin Seeley on the starting grid.* (B.R. Nicholls)

Above right *Fancy meeting you here! Giacomo Agostini (left) and Mike (Seeley) chat on the grid at the 1969 Mallory Park 'Race of the Year' meeting. Number 44 is Ken Redfern (750 Norton), and 22 is John Cooper (Seeley). Ago won the race with Mike fifth, first of the singles home. Earlier he had been third in the 500cc race.* (B.R. Nicholls)

Right *Battling it out in the 1969 Mallory Park 'Race of the Year', Mike on his 500cc Seeley leads Malcolm Uphill (700cc Metisse) and Dave Croxford (500cc Seeley) as they accelerate from the hairpin.* (B.R. Nicholls)

CHAPTER 8

Daytona and the Island

Fate conspired to tempt Hailwood back into the big-time almost immediately. While he was on holiday, first in South Africa and then in Switzerland, the British BSA-Triumph group were planning an ambitious assault on America's most prestigious motorcycle race – the world famous Daytona 200. Run under the auspices of the American Motorcycle Association – not at that time affiliated to the Fédération Internationale Motocycliste which controlled the sport virtually world-wide – this event had previously been limited to road-ster-based machines with a maximum capacity of 500cc for overhead-valve and 750cc for side-valve engines. But under pressure from the growing number of motorcycle importers these rules were modified for 1970. The bikes raced still had to be powered by what were basically sports machine engines, but the capacity limit was now 750cc for all types of power unit. By a happy chance

Mike (BSA) leads in the early stages of the 1970 Daytona 200, pursued by Gary Nixon (Triumph), Cal Rayborn (Harley-Davidson), eventual winner Dick Mann (Honda), and Kel Carruthers (Yamaha). Mike retired with plug trouble. (Mick Woollett)

this change coincided with a boom in the American motorcycle market and a drive by BSA-Triumph to promote sales of their recently introduced 750cc three-cylinder BSA Rocket and Triumph Trident superbikes.

Realising that a Daytona win would be the finest possible publicity for the new triples, the British group commissioned their talented development engineer Doug Hele to build a batch of suitably modified machines for the race. Fortunately Hele had a racing background. He had worked under the legendary Joe Craig at Nortons in their glory days in the early 1950s, had developed the racing Manx Nortons after Craig left; and had built the twin-cylinder Norton 'Domiracer' on which Australian Tom Phillis had finished third in the 1961 Senior TT. Fortunately he also had plenty of Daytona experience. Twin-cylinder 500cc Triumphs which he had developed had won the big race in 1966 and 1967, ridden by Buddy Elmore and Gary Nixon, and Doug had been at the Florida track on both occasions. Now he was looking for world-class road racers to team with BSA-Triumph's established American stars.

Obviously Hailwood's name came up when riders

were discussed, and Hele delegated Triumph tester and racer Percy Tait to first find him and then persuade him to join the team. Percy tracked him down to his flat in Heston, near London's Heathrow airport. 'He agreed straight away and money was never mentioned,' recalls Tait, now a successful car dealer with a chain of Midland Suzuki agencies. So just weeks after the readers of *Motor Cycle* had voted Mike their 'Man of the Sixties' by the massive margin of 82 per cent to Phil Read's six, they read of his unexpected return to racing.

At first it was thought that he would ride a Triumph, and our story in *Motor Cycle* at the end of February reflected this. Under the headline 'Triumph bid for Hailwood', the story read: 'Mike Hailwood is almost certain to race one of the 160mph [257.44kph] three-cylinder works Triumphs in the Daytona 200 on March 15. Despite saying barely ten days ago that he had no plans whatsoever to race motorcycles he has been entered for the American classic by the Meriden factory along with works tester Percy Tait.' Asked for his comments, Mike had replied: 'I'm quite prepared to go but have put on so much weight that I don't know whether I'll be able to get into my leathers.'

He need not have worried. A brand-new set of leathers, luxury hotel accommodation, transport by limousine, and gun-toting security guards were all part of a lavish presence at Daytona that year. Factory politics decided that Mike should in fact race a BSA, teaming with Americans Dave Aldana and Jim Rice, while their compatriots Gary Nixon, Gene Romero, and Don Castro raced the Triumphs, with Tait in support. It promised to be a fantastic race, contested by seven of the world's biggest manufacturers, with Honda, Suzuki, Yamaha, Kawasaki, and Harley-Davidson, as well as BSA-Triumph, all fielding works teams on the fastest racing motorcycles ever seen.

Hailwood wasted no time. He qualified second fastest with a lap at 152.90mph (246.02kph) around the speed bowl, beaten only by Triumph's Romero, and took an early lead in the race which he held until lap ten of the 53-lap 200-mile (321.8km) event. Then a misfire set in and became so severe that Mike retired at the pits. The problem was later traced to overheating which had 'cooked' a sparking plug. There had simply been insuffi-

cient time to fully test the new engine under all conditions, and when ridden hard over a long distance it had overheated. With Hailwood out victory went to veteran Dick Mann, who nursed his Honda CB750 to victory after his three team-mates had all retired with camshaft drive problems. It was touch and go at the finish with Mann just ahead of Romero and Castro on their Triumphs.

Hailwood then flew home to open the Swedish motorcycle show in Stockholm in early April, and in May he crossed to the Isle of Man to spectate at the TT. Even that year, nine years later, his single cylinder lap record of 101.64mph (163.54kph) on a Bill Lacey Norton remained unbeaten, though Alan Barnett on a Seeley got close at 101.02mph (162.54kph). Mike contested no British or Continental races during 1970, not even the Mallory Park 'Race of the Year', where he had had his sole British outing the previous year. But he was there spectating. He denied rumours that he would be joining Benelli for 1971 but did not rule out the possibility that he might race bikes again, possibly at Daytona. This was confirmed in January 1971 when it was reported that Peter Thornton, the BSA-Triumph group's big-spending boss in America, had invited Mike – then on holiday in South Africa – to race at Daytona again. In reply to a cable from *Motor Cycle* asking if he had accepted, Mike replied laconically: 'Yes thanks'.

A week later there was speculation that he might race the big BSA in British events, and possibly a racing version of the recently announced 350cc double overhead camshaft Fury twin. But in early February he scotched these rumours, and a big-money offer from Benelli, by signing a car racing contract with Team Surtees. Speaking about the Benelli offer, Mike said: 'The money was very tempting but there are lots of reasons why I decided against bikes. For one thing you can't be away from bikes for three years and hope to come back and pick up where you left off.' Which, in the light of what happened seven years later, is an interesting comment!

For 1971 the BSA-Triumph racing triples featured a number of minor improvements and one major one – the fitting of a double disc front brake in place of the massive Fontana drum used previously. Mike had experience of disc brakes, having tried a Colin Lyster experimental set-up on his 350cc Honda in 1967 and a single Lockheed on his 500cc Honda the following year, but the sheer power of the twin Lockheeds on his BSA caught him out. They locked the front wheel as he slammed the brakes on at 150mph (241.35kph) coming off the banked track and on to the infield 'road race' section, and he parted company with the BSA at around 120mph (193kph) before tumbling to a halt on the grassy infield. Luckily he escaped with no more than heavy bruising and reported that he had been caught out by the lack of feel of the new brakes. But typically he blamed himself for the crash and made his comment with a grin on his face.

That year the starting order qualifying procedure had been changed. Instead of a lap of the speed-bowl riders had to complete a single lap of the actual racing circuit, part bowl part flat infield. Triumph's new recruit, Paul Smart, set the pace at 105.80mph (170.23kph) ahead of Harley-Davidson's Cal Rayborn and Mark Brelsford, and BSA's Don Emde, with Mike only fifth fastest at 105.06mph (169.04kph). Asked how he felt about this he replied with typical candour: 'Embarrassed. I found it very difficult to just go out and do a single lap. I needed two or three to get into the swing of things.'

From the start of the race Gary Fisher shot ahead on a Honda CB750, leaving Mike to 'get into the swing of things' amid the pursuing pack of Smart, Rayborn, and previous year's winner Mann, who had rejoined BSA and was riding a bike identical to Mike's. Before long Fisher was eliminated by a broken camshaft drive chain and Rayborn pulled into the pits with a gearbox problem, while the experienced Mann – a competitor at Daytona since the days of the old half-beach, half-road circuit – let the duelling pair of Hailwood and Smart pull away in the lead.

The two British riders put on a great show, but just when it seemed that Hailwood had the upper hand his engine started to misfire and he pulled into the pits having completed only 15 laps, just over a quarter of the race distance. Whereas the previous year his problem was traced to the selection of the wrong grade of plug this time a valve had partly burned away. Smart now led the race, but Mann, who had conserved his engine,

speeded up and closed the gap. Then, just when it seemed we might see a fight to the finish, Smart ran into piston trouble and, with his Triumph misfiring, he retired after completing 42 of the 53 laps. This left Mann to win ahead of fellow Americans Gene Romero (Triumph) and Don Emde (BSA), who made it a 1–2–3 success for the three-cylinder British bikes.

Despite a busy season driving the Team Surtees cars in Formula 5000 and Formula 1, including a fourth place in the Italian Grand Prix, Mike still hankered after bike racing and in July he confirmed a rumour that he might ride in Mallory Park's 'Race of the Year' in September, saying: 'I've been thinking of having a go at Mallory if I can find a suitable bike.' He then had a good offer to ride in the ACU's international meeting at Silverstone, including a Formula 750 event on 22 August. Obviously his first choice was a BSA but by that time the British group was in deep financial trouble. A £3.3m loss for the financial year 1970–1 had just been announced and the racing budget had been drastically cut. This meant no BSA for Mike and a hurried search for a replacement. He contacted his old friends at Ducati who he knew were developing a Formula 750 racer, and they agreed to send a machine and mechanics for him to try at Silverstone the week before the event.

Engineer Fabio Taglioni's now famous vee-twin, the dominant force in World Superbike racing during the 1990s, was in its infancy at the time, and after a disappointing test session Mike rejected it in favour of a brand-new works 350cc TR Yamaha twin. This arrived at the circuit on Saturday – but Mike did not. He was at Oulton Park practising for a car race, and the only chance he got to try the bike before racing it at Silverstone was during a ten-minute 'warm up' session on the Sunday morning.

The first appearance of Hailwood on a British circuit for nearly two years, combined with the first major bike meeting at Silverstone for six, attracted a massive crowd to the Northamptonshire circuit. Mike's first outing was in the 350cc race when, unfamiliar with the Yamaha starting technique, he was almost last away. After two laps he was back in 18th place. Then he got into his stride and delighted the crowd as he cut through the field to finish a fine fourth, beaten only by Giacomo Agostini (MV Agusta), Jarno Saarinen (Yamaha), and John Cooper (Yamsel) – all established stars riding at the top of their form. In the Formula 750 race Mike was again fourth, the first 350cc home behind the works BSA-Triumph 750cc three-cylinder racers of Smart, Tait, and Ray Pickrell. Asked for his comments, Mike replied: 'It was great. I really enjoyed it. Passing Phil Read in the 350cc race really made my day.' Asked about the Yamaha, he said: 'It didn't handle well enough. This isn't surprising because it is only three weeks old and has never been raced before. It just needs a bit of sorting out.' Questioned about a full-time return to bike racing he said: 'It's too early to say yet. It's true I need the money but I'll have to see how I go'.

Mike's appearance at Silverstone had miffed the Mallory organisers and at first they rescinded their invitation for him to compete at their 'Race of the Year' meeting in September. But his Silverstone performance and the reaction of the fans forced a re-think and a deal was struck before Mike flew out to a meeting at Pesaro to earn big money by racing a year-old 350cc Benelli into second place behind Agostini. In fact Mallory proved a disappointment. Hailwood could only finish fourth in the 350cc race and was never in the hunt in the feature event, retiring from tenth place with piston ring trouble. But the crowd still had plenty to cheer, because this was the famous race in which Cooper, on Doug Hele's latest 750cc BSA, fought and won a great duel with Agostini on his works 500cc MV Agusta.

There was a rumour Yamaha wanted Hailwood to help them develop a four-cylinder bike for an attack on the 500cc class, but late in 1971 John Surtees blocked any possibility of this when he agreed a car-racing contract with Mike for 1972. This specifically banned all motorcycle racing. Reporting this in *Motor Cycle* under the headline 'Hailwood quits – by order', I wrote: 'Former motorcycle World Champion John Surtees has vetoed further bike rides for Mike Hailwood. Following a successful season in Surtees cars ... Hailwood has been offered a contract by Surtees for 1972. "But it means no more bikes", said Hailwood: "You could say that John has made up my mind for me."' It seemed that motorcycle racing and Mike Hailwood had finally

parted company after a long and lingering farewell that had really started four years previously when Honda pulled out of the World Championships at the end of 1967.

Mike won the European Formula 2 championship for Team Surtees in 1972 and drove a Surtees to second place in that year's Formula 1 Italian Grand Prix. The following year the Surtees cars were not competitive but Hailwood hit the headlines when he risked his life to pull Clay Regazzoni from his blazing BRM during the South African Grand Prix. His bravery won him the George Medal.

Mike's performances in the Surtees had meanwhile caught the eye of the McLaren team and he switched to them in 1974. Immediately competitive, he scored points in four of the first ten World Championship rounds before he crashed at high speed at the Nürburgring in Germany. His car slammed into the trackside Armco barrier after landing awkwardly after a jump and he suffered a very badly broken right leg. Initially he hoped to be fit for the 1975 season but when it became obvious that this was out of the question he decided to make a clean break. He married his partner Pauline and emigrated to New Zealand with daughter Michelle and son David. He flew back to Britain to attend the 1975 TT and was given a tremendous ovation by a crowd of 2,000 when he was installed as president of the TT Supporters' Club, but little was heard of him for the next two years. Then he turned up at the 1977 British Motorcycle Grand Prix, the first mainland meeting to have World Championship status following the relegation of the Isle of Man TT. He was already something of a curiosity and the caption to a picture of him in *Motor Cycle* read: 'The old and the new. Mike Hailwood who flew from his new home in New Zealand to Silverstone, looks pensive as Johnny Cecotto prepares for the fray'.

But Mike was not finished yet. Far from it. He had flown to England and was at Silverstone in mid-August as the first step in a plan to make a comeback at the 1978 TT. Bored with life in New Zealand and angered by criticism of his beloved TT circuit, he hankered to have another crack around the famous island lap. There was, of course, another dimension – money. Having lost

World Championship status, the organisers now had to tempt the stars with big money. It was said that they had paid Phil Read £12,000 to race there in 1977. Mike and his friend and adviser Ted Macauley realised that if the organiser could sign Mike for 1978 their publicity problems for that year would be over. They met Vernon Cooper, chairman of the organising committee, at Silverstone, and it was all settled in just ten minutes.

The deal was announced to readers of *Motor Cycle* in the 3 September issue under the headline 'Hailwood set for '78 TT', with the story: 'Mike Hailwood, winner of a record 12 TT races, is to race in the Isle of Man next June. Hailwood, who last rode in the Island back in 1967 when he fought and won an epic duel with Giacomo Agostini, confirmed his plan at the weekend.' Said the 37-year-old former World Champion: 'I'm not making a comeback, just returning after eleven years! I've always liked riding round the Island; I think I'll be competitive.' He said he had no definite plans about bikes but hoped that Yamaha would support him by lending him 250 and 500cc machines.

He then crossed to the Isle of Man, where he did a lap on a TZ750 Yamaha fitted with a camera before flying back to New Zealand. The question now was just how seriously should we take this comeback? He was overweight, balding, partly crippled by his 1974 Formula 1 crash, and had not raced in the TT for 11 years. He would also be 38 when he faced the starter. It was a tall order, but in our hearts those of us who knew him were confident. For this was no mere man, this was Mike Hailwood, blessed with such natural talent that mere age was unlikely to diminish it. He was a link with the past. We had grown up under his spell and desperately wanted him to succeed. But could he?

In October came the news that he had signed to ride a 900cc Ducati in the Formula One TT for Sports Motor Cycles of Manchester, whose director Steve Wynne reported that they would be building a bike specially for Mike, who had been impressed when he visited their camp at Silverstone. Meanwhile on the other side of the world Mike was undergoing a rigorous 'get fit' campaign and at the end of October he rode in his first serious race for six years when he competed in Australia. The event was the Castrol Six-Hour produc-

tion machine race at Amaroo Park and he and co-rider Jim Scaysbrook finished sixth on a 750cc Ducati.

At the end of the year we heard that experienced Rhodesian mechanic Nobby Clark, who had recently left the Yamaha set-up (where he had looked after Agostini's bikes), would be helping Mike at the TT. His brief would be to prepare the Yamahas that the Japanese factory's Amsterdam-based team had agreed to provide. This tie-up and Martini sponsorship were confirmed at a lavish press conference in London in January 1978. This was the first time Martini had been involved in motorcycle sport and during the conference Mike's precise plans were announced. In addition to the Ducati he would race Yamahas in the Junior (a 250cc race), Senior (500cc), and Classic (1,000cc) TTs. Looking far trimmer than he had in September, Mike said he was not out to win but was coming back because he loved the TT circuit and wanted to race on it again. He then flew out to Barbados to visit his terminally ill father Stan, the man who had done so much to further his career and who sadly died a few weeks later aged 75.

From the Caribbean Mike flew home to New Zealand and in late March competed on a TZ750 Yamaha at the Bathurst Easter meeting in Australia, finishing ninth after suffering plug trouble in a rain-soaked race. He went on to team with Scaysbrook on the 750cc Ducati in a three-hour race at Adelaide in which they finished seventh after twice running out of fuel.

He arrived back in the UK in April and crossed to the Isle of Man on 22 May to start his final preparations, saying: 'There have been so many alterations to the track that I need plenty of practice to refresh myself. Don't expect miracles.' By this time I had organised a deal with Mike for him to write an exclusive weekly article for *Motor Cycle* during the TT period. In effect this meant me interviewing him and getting his thoughts down on paper. In his first column he said that the biggest change he had found was in tyres and brakes: 'Tremendous grip and fantastic stopping power compared to 1967 so I've not only got to re-learn the circuit, I've got to learn to ride all over again.' He complained that practising had been cut to six hours, which meant just 90 minutes on each bike, and said people were taking his comeback too seriously. Commenting on how he would go, he said: 'Frankly I haven't a clue. I'm happy with my physical condition but then I always did find the TT more of a mentally demanding race than a physical one.'

The doubters had begun to revise their ideas when he bettered the Formula One lap record during training with a round at 111mph (178.6kph) on the Ducati. This was the fastest for the class and made him favourite for the race. His form on the bigger Yamahas had been impressive too. On the 500cc, the bike raced by Agostini the previous year, he was fourth fastest at 107.75mph (173.37kph), while on a brand-new TZ750E, his mount for the Classic TT, he was third best at 112.36mph (180.79kph). Only in the 250cc class did Mike fail to figure among the fastest. First he suffered gearbox problems and then, when he went out during the final session to do a fast lap, he slid off at Braddan Bridge. That was on the Saturday morning – just hours before the start of the Formula One TT!

Confident after his record-breaking practice lap, Mike's tactics in the Formula One race were simple: 'I decided to ride at only nine-tenths and to see how things were going when I got to my signalling station at the Gooseneck. If I was leading there I could slow down even more. If on the other hand Phil [Read] was leading then I'd have to speed up a bit.' In fact he led the race there by a few seconds, not from Read but from Tom Herron on a Honda prepared by London dealers Mocheck. Mike responded with a record lap at 110.62mph (177.99kph), and when the pursuing Ulsterman retired on the third lap with bike problems, he was left to cruise home to victory, actually passing Read (Honda) – who had started 50 seconds ahead of him – in the process. 'I must admit I nearly had a little cry, a little weep, when I got off the bike and the realisation that I had won hit me,' said Mike, adding: 'You know the last time I raced here we were all wearing pudding basin helmets!'

Monday's 500cc Senior TT, however, was a great disappointment. Mike insisted after practising that mechanics Nobby Clark and Jerry Wood change the Yamaha steering damper for a Kawasaki one. It proved a mistake. After a slow start – his crippled leg making it difficult for him to push-start a heavy bike – he finished the first lap in fourth place, only 24 seconds behind the leader and eventual winner Herron (Suzuki). But then the damper broke, slowing Mike and forcing him to make a long pit stop to have it repaired. By the time he re-started he was out of the running, but he kept going nonetheless – only to run out of fuel on the last lap on the Mountain. He borrowed some from a spectator and eventually finished 28th, but having broken the rules he did not accept the silver replica to which he would normally have been entitled.

He fared a little better in the Junior 250cc race on the Wednesday. The problem was that he had done only two laps on the bike during practice and had to learn to ride it as the race went on. Added to that he only had a small fuel tank and had to make two refuelling stops. He eventually finished 12th in a wet race but was among the handful of riders who lapped at over 100mph (161kph). He admitted after the race that he had used it as extra practice for the climax of the week, the Classic TT. After that third-fastest practice lap he was confident he could do well, but his hopes ended in sad disappointment when a piston broke after just half a lap. It was a dismal end to a week that had started so brilliantly. 'What a bastard!' said Mike. 'I've never been so disappointed in all my life. I was even more disappointed than I was at Monza in 1967 when my Honda ate its gearbox and cost me the World Championship.' But could he have won the race? 'I don't know,' he admitted. 'Mick Grant was going awfully fast but I'm confident I could have finished second.'

Summing up his TT comeback in his column for *Motor Cycle*, he said: 'I'm glad it's all over. The riding part of it wasn't hard. In fact just about the only time I could relax and enjoy myself was when I was on the bikes. It was the rest of the performance that got on my nerves. I must have given umpteen million interviews and I couldn't set foot outside the hotel without attracting attention … basically it was a bloody silly idea that turned out reasonably well.'

Two days after the Classic TT he was at Mallory Park, where he faced the local 'scratchers' on an English short circuit for the first time since 1971. This type of racing required a very different technique to the Isle of Man and one which did not suit the long-wheelbase Ducati. Added to that, Mike had only time for two ten-minute practice sessions and then made a slow start. Tenth into the first corner, he fought his way through to win – with the fastest lap of the race – from John Cowie (Kawasaki) and Read (Honda). It was a win that put a grin back on his face. 'It proves I can still scratch a bit,' he commented on the rostrum.

He had two more outings on British circuits that year – at Donington in July and Silverstone in August. At both he rode only the 860cc Ducati in Formula One events. He crashed at Donington when he was caught out by a slick front tyre he was using for the first time, and finished third at Silverstone behind Cowie (Kawasaki) and Herron (Honda). After the latter event Mike said: 'That's it for this year. I rode as hard as I could but the old Duke just didn't have enough grunt to beat the four-cylinder machines.' Asked about his plans Mike said he would be racing a Ducati in the Castrol six-hours in Australia in October, but regarding 1979 admitted that 'I honestly don't know – you'll have to wait and see.'

The Australian outing proved a disappointment, with co-rider Scaysbrook crashing, but at about the same time Mike's friend and mentor Macauley confirmed that there were plans afoot for Hailwood to make a final TT appearance in 1979: 'He would like to race in the TT again because he felt that he disappointed a lot of people when bike trouble forced him out of the Classic TT on the first lap.' It was quickly confirmed that he would again race a Ducati in the Formula One race and it was at first assumed that he would also ride Yamahas in the other classes. Then in November Chris Carter wrote in *Motor Cycle*: 'Funny how the obvious is sometimes overlooked. For instance Mike Hailwood on a works Suzuki for the 1979 TT! No-one is owning up to anything but we are pretty certain approaches have been made'. After four months of rumour and counter rumour the deal was struck. Mike would ride a works four-cylinder 500cc Suzuki, with the full support of the British-based Texaco Heron Team Suzuki – who also ran the Japanese factory's Grand Prix team – in the Senior and Classic races.

While that side of things was cut-and-dried the Ducati situation worsened. In April Mike had his first European outing of 1979 when he rode the latest works Ducati in a test session at Misano. It ended disastrously when he crashed at high speed following gearbox problems. He was knocked out for a few seconds and the incident so frightened the Italian factory that they pulled out of the TT. Sports Motor Cycles of Manchester then took over, bought the works bikes from the factory, and entered Mike in the race as they had the previous year. Tests with the Suzuki went far better. After his first session at Donington Mike reported: 'What a nice surprise the Suzuki is turning out to be. Both Barry Sheene and Steve Parrish warned me it didn't handle, had a hinge in the middle and was generally a bit of a handful … but to my delight it was fine'.

By contrast the Ducati simply would not handle during TT practice until the team reverted to a year-old frame – by which time Mike had found that he could not match the speed of the improved 996cc four-cylinder Hondas. Curiously the bike was nowhere near as fast as the previous year and was unable to match his 1968 lap times. Mike battled to hold third place in the race until a series of problems hit him on the sixth and final round. First top gear went missing, then an exhaust pipe broke, and finally the battery came loose and the engine cut out completely a few miles from the flag. After coasting to a standstill Mike managed a repair, restarted the Ducati, and finished a very weary fifth in a race won by Alex George (Honda).

Two days later in the 500cc Senior TT it was a very different matter. Despite only doing five practice laps on the Suzuki – a 1978 works model – Mike was confident. He took it easy on the first lap to get the feel of the bike, which he found totally different to the Ducati, then speeded up and won at a record 111.75mph (179.81kph), with a record lap at 114.02mph (183.46kph) also in the bag. Reporting for *Motor Cycle*, I wrote: 'Hailwood has done it. On Monday mighty Mike blasted his way to his fourteenth TT win … Yet this incredible superstar was completely relaxed at the end of the six-lap race. Looking ready for another 226 miles [363.63km], Mike the Bike said: "No problems at all. The Suzuki was perfect, it went like a dream. I'm looking forward to racing it again in Friday's Classic."'

In fact Friday's race was a classic in every way. In my race report I wrote of the 'sheer sustained fury' as Hailwood on his 500cc Suzuki two-stroke slugged it out with Alex George on his mighty 1,000cc Honda four-stroke. After five nerve-jangling laps they rocketed into the last with Mike leading by less than a second! Baulked on a couple of occasions, Mike lost precious seconds on that final lap and George rode superbly to win at 113.08mph (181.95kph) – the fastest TT ever. Afterwards Mike said: 'Alex went too quick for me. I didn't want to stick my neck out any farther. That's the first time I've ever finished second in a TT.' In his column for *Motor Cycle* he wrote: 'I have finally and irrevocably retired from TT racing – about time too. After all I will be 40 next year and it is hard for me to believe I rode in my first TT exactly 21 years ago – in 1958.'

However, that was not his last race. Mike had entered on the Ducati for the post-TT Mallory meeting and on the Suzuki for a Donington Park meeting scheduled for early July. At Mallory he was unable to race the Ducati because it had been badly damaged when George Fogarty (father of Superbike World Champion Carl) had crashed in the Classic TT. Instead he rode a Paul Dunstall GS1000 Suzuki but was never among the leaders and retired with front brake problems. And, sad to say, although he was at Donington and did a lap with circuit-owner Tom Wheatcroft in a pre-war super-charged Bentley, he was unable to race. He had badly broken a collarbone when he crashed at high-speed that same morning, but despite the pain was determined to at least show the crowd that he was there.

The Hailwood family had meanwhile moved back to Britain from New Zealand and Mike had recently opened a motorcycle shop in Birmingham in partner-ship with 1970 250cc World Champion Rod Gould. It proved to be in the wrong place at the wrong time. Situated under Birmingham's 'spaghetti junction' motorway complex it was hard to find and the two-wheeler trade was in deep recession.

Then, less than two years after he had ridden his last motorcycle race, Mike and his daughter Michelle were killed in a car accident. They had set out in the family Rover saloon to get a fish and chip supper from a 'chippy' near their home in Tamworth-in-Arden when a truck they were passing on a dual carriageway did an illegal U-turn across the central reservation.

Mike clung to life for a few days before he succumbed to his injuries. The world's most famous racing motor-cyclist had been killed by a truck-driver's moment of carelessness.

Two veterans of hundreds of races chatting at the 1970 'Race of the Year' at Mallory Park – Mike (left) and Gary Nixon, who twice won the American Motorcycle Association's national championship. (Mick Woollett)

Above far left *A full-face Bell helmet in place of the 'pudding basin' he had used for 13 years, and coloured leathers in place of his usual sombre black make Mike hard to recognise on the BSA as he accelerates from the infield on to the banking at Daytona in 1970. (Mick Woollett)*

Above left *Daytona 1970, and Mike gets ready to practise on one of the fabulously fast 750cc three-cylinder BSAs, aided by an American mechanic. (Mick Woollett)*

Left *Two champions meet at Daytona 1970 as Mike (left),*

nine-times *a road racing World Champion, chats to four-times speedway World Champion Barry Briggs. (Mick Woollett)*

Above *Impressive line-up of 750cc three-cylinder BSA racers at Daytona in 1971. Left to right: Don Emde, Mike Hailwood, and Dick Mann, who won the race for the British factory that year. Note that Emde, the junior member of the team, is on a 1970 spec bike with Fontana drum brake while Hailwood and Mann have the new bikes with disc brakes and 'letterbox' air-scoop below the front number. (Mick Woollett)*

Left *Twelve months on from his Daytona début, Mike looks very much more professional in this shot from the 1971 race, which he led on his Doug Hele-developed 750cc BSA Rocket 3 until a valve broke.* (Mick Woollett)

Below *Duel in the sun as two Englishmen battle for the lead at Daytona in 1971. Paul Smart, who had been fastest in qualifying, leads on a factory 750cc three-cylinder Triumph chased by Mike, who raced the near identical BSA triple.* (Mick Woollett)

Right *Mike in action on a 350cc Yamaha at the international meeting at Silverstone in August 1971. It was his first British meeting for nearly two years and he took two fourth places.* (Mick Woollett)

Below right *Mike's second and final meeting in England in 1971 was at the Mallory Park 'Race of the Year' in September. Here he waits on a 350cc Yamaha with works mechanics Jerry Wood (left) and Nobby Clark in attendance. He retired from the big race with piston ring problems but took a fourth place in the 350cc race.* (Mick Woollett)

Above *Mallory Park, September 1971, and Mike leads the 350cc race from Jarno Saarinen (Yamaha, 6) and Derek Chatterton (Yamaha, 24). Mike finished fourth in this, his last British meeting for seven years.* (Wolfgang Gruber)

Left *1976 Formula 1 World Champion James Hunt rides pillion with Mike at Brands Hatch in April 1974.* (B.R. Nicholls)

Above right *Two great lovers of the Isle of Man TT races meet on the Island in 1975. Geoff Duke (left), winner of five TTs, watches while Mike, still recovering from the serious car racing accident suffered the previous year, signs autographs.* (Mick Woollett)

Right *Although still recovering from the crash that ended his car racing career, Mike could not resist doing a lap of the TT circuit when he visited the Isle of Man in 1975. Here he is seen on a borrowed Yamaha twin.* (Mick Woollett)

Left *Mike (right) was already planning his TT comeback when this picture of him with the author was taken at Silverstone in 1977.* (B.R. Nicholls)

Below *The Hailwood family in 1978. Left to right: Pauline, David, Michelle, and Mike.* (Courtesy of Pauline Hailwood)

Right *His first TT for 11 years, the 1978 750cc Formula One race. Mike, on the Sports Motor Cycles vee-twin Ducati, is beaten away from the clutch start by Ian Richards (Kawasaki).* (Mick Woollett)

Below right *Man and machine in perfect harmony. This impressive shot shows Mike hurling the big Ducati round Quarter Bridge during his winning ride in the 1978 750cc Formula One TT.* (Mick Woollett)

Left *Here comes the winner – and cameras click as Mike rounds Governors Bridge on the big Ducati during his triumphant ride in the 1978 750cc Formula One TT.* (Mick Woollett)

Right *Mike in the winner's enclosure after the 1978 Formula One TT. The hand he is shaking belongs to runner-up John Williams, while the girls trying to get in on the act are nothing to do with Hailwood. They represent Champion and Dunlop.* (Mick Woollett)

Below *You cannot get closer to the action than the spectators who line the circuit at Creg-ny-Baa as Mike flashes by on his 500cc Yamaha during the 1978 Senior TT. A broken steering damper put paid to his chances.* (Mick Woollett)

Above *Serious leg injuries suffered when he crashed in the German car Grand Prix in 1974 made it difficult for Mike to push-start a bike. Luckily for him the Formula One event was a clutch-start, but here he struggles to get his Yamaha to fire as he sets off alongside Takazumi Katayama in the 1978 250cc TT. (Mick Woollett)*

Right *Mike looks pensive as mechanic Nobby Clark warms up his Yamaha TZ750E before the start of the 1978 Classic TT with a second mechanic, Jerry Wood, looking on. (Mick Woollett)*

Left *Short circuit action in the post-TT Mallory Park meeting in June 1978, with Mike (Ducati) leading Phil Read (Honda) around the hairpin. After winning the race he said: 'It proves I can still scratch a bit!' (B.R. Nicholls)*

Left *Mike, by now aged 39, cranks the 500cc works Suzuki into Creg-ny-Baa during his winning ride in the 1979 Senior TT. It was his 14th and last TT win, and during the race he pushed the lap record up to 114.02mph (183.46kph).* (B.R. Nicholls)

Right *Whoops! Mike puts out a steadying foot as he nearly drops the works four-cylinder two-stroke Suzuki at Governors Bridge during the 1979 Senior TT.* (B.R. Nicholls)

Below *One of Mike's last appearances at a grand prix circuit on a works Honda was at the 1980 Dutch TT. Here he does a parade lap on a restored 297cc six-cylinder machine. The date was 29 June – less than nine months before he was fatally injured in a road accident while driving a car.* (Mick Woollett)

Race results 1957–79

In this section I have tried to list every single meeting and every race that Mike Hailwood rode in during his astounding 23-year motorcycle racing career. I am confident of the accuracy of most of this information, but some of the dates of his South African and Australian meetings have proved difficult to verify.

Each meeting constitutes a separate entry complete with date, followed by a listing of the classes he rode in and the makes of machine he rode (with capacity where this differed by more than ten per cent from the permitted engine size – for example where he rode 203cc MV in 250cc races). This is followed by a comment where relevant, and the race result. The comments include reasons for retirement or poor performance, who beat him in important races, and record laps with speeds where these were particularly significant (though not all record laps are noted). No race records are included here, nor are the results of the qualifying heats which were part of the British scene in the early days.

The following five abbreviations are used: DNF – Did not finish; DNP – Finished but not placed; DNS – Did not start; ET – Engine trouble; F1 – Motorcycle Formula One. It should be noted that two different motorcycle Formula One classes existed during Hailwood's career. The first, in 1958 and 1959, catered for 350 and 500cc production racing machines such as the Manx Norton and 7R AJS. The second, in 1978 and 1979, was limited to race-tuned sports machines with a 750cc limit the first year which was increased to 1,000cc in 1979.

Race	Machine	Comment	Placing

1957

Oulton Park, 22 April

150cc	125 MV	First ever race	11

Castle Combe, 27 April

125cc	MV		4
250cc	175 MV		5

Brands Hatch, 12 May

200cc	175 MV		3

Blandford, 10 June

50cc	Itom		3
125cc	MV	First win	1
250cc	175 MV		5

Scarborough, 14 June

250cc	175 MV	Crashed, minor injuries	DNF

Silverstone, 6 July

First 250cc	203 MV		2
Second 250cc	203 MV		2

Snetterton, 14 July

125cc	MV		3
250cc	203 MV	First 250 win	1

Brands Hatch, 21 July

200cc	175 MV		2

Rhydymwyn, 27 July

150cc	125 MV		1
250cc	203 MV	First double win	1

Oulton Park, 3 August

50cc	Itom		2
125cc	MV		3
250cc	203 MV	Crashed, broke collarbone	DNF

Brands Hatch, 8 September

200cc	175 MV		1
250cc	175 MV		2

Scarborough, 14 September

250cc	203 MV	First international meeting	3

Pietermaritzburg, South Africa, 15 December

250cc	NSU	First race in South Africa	1

1958

Port Elizabeth 200, South Africa, 1 January

250cc	NSU	Record lap, 90.76mph (146.03kph)	1

Pietermaritzburg, South Africa, 19 January

250cc	NSU	Record lap	1

Pietermaritzburg, South Africa, 16 February

250cc	NSU		1

Pretoria, Grand Central, South Africa, 2 March

250cc	NSU		1
350cc	Norton	Norton début, ET	DNF

Port Elizabeth, St Albans, South Africa, 16 March

350cc	Norton	ET	DNF

Cape Town, Easter River, South Africa, 29 March

250cc	NSU	Record lap	1
H'cap	250 NSU		2

Brands Hatch, 4 April

200cc	175 MV	Record lap	1
250cc	NSU	Minter (REG) won	2

Crystal Palace, 7 April

200cc	MV	Record lap	1
250cc	NSU		1

Mallory Park, 13 April

250cc	NSU	Purslow (NSU) won	2
350cc	Norton	UK Norton début	5
500cc	Norton	500cc début	DNP

Silverstone, 19 April

125cc	MV		1
250cc	NSU		DNF

Castle Combe, 26 April

125cc	MV	Contested four major races	1
250cc	NSU		1
350cc	Norton		6
500cc	Norton		6

Brands Hatch, 4 May

200cc	MV		1
250cc	NSU		1
350cc	Norton	First 350cc win	1
500cc	Norton	Crashed when sixth	DNF

Aintree, 10 May

200cc	MV	Purslow (Ducati) won	2
250cc	NSU	Purslow (NSU) won	2

Cookstown, 14 May

200cc	MV	Handicap, won from scratch	1
250cc	NSU	Retired lap 2, ET	DNF

North West 200, 17 May

250cc	NSU	Miller (NSU) won	2

Brands Hatch, 26 May

250cc	NSU		1
350cc	Norton		1
500cc	Norton	Anderson (Norton) won	2

Isle of Man TT, 2 June

350cc	Norton	First TT mountain circuit	12

Isle of Man TT, 4 June

125cc	Paton	First TT Clypse circuit	7
250cc	NSU	Beaten only by works MVs	3

Isle of Man TT, 6 June

500cc	Norton	Finished all four TTs	13

Mallory Park, 7 June

250cc	NSU		1
350cc	Norton		1
500cc	Norton	ET	DNF

Scarborough, 13 June

150cc	125 Paton	Carburettor trouble	DNF
250cc	NSU		1

Snetterton, 14 June

125cc	MV	Record lap	1
250cc	NSU	Record lap	1
350cc	Norton	Record lap	1
500cc	Norton	Record lap	2

Thruxton, 21 June

500-m sports machine race	650 Triumph	Hailwood and D.F. Shorey	1

Dutch TT, Assen, 28 June

125cc	Ducati	First Continental meeting	10
250cc	NSU		4
350cc	Norton		5

Castle Combe, 12 July

125cc	MV		1
250cc	NSU		1
350cc	Norton		1
500cc	Norton	Oiled plug at start	DNF
H'cap	250 NSU		1

German GP, Nürburgring, 20 July

250cc	NSU	Front brake trouble	DNF
350cc	Norton		4

Swedish GP, Hedemora, 26 July

250cc	NSU	Fugner (MZ) won	2
350cc	Norton		3

Crystal Palace, 4 August

125cc	MV		1
250cc	NSU		1
350cc	Norton		6
500cc	Norton		5

Race	Machine	Comment	Placing
Ulster GP, Dundrod, 9 August			
250cc	NSU	Slid off, wet track	DNF
350cc	Norton		8
Aberdare Park, 23 August			
125cc	MV		1
250cc	NSU		1
350cc	Norton		3
Brands Hatch, 24 August			
200cc	125 Ducati	Chadwick (175 MV) won	2
250cc	NSU		1
350cc	Norton	Minter (Norton) won	2
Zandvoort, Holland, 31 August			
125cc	Ducati	Scheidhauer (Ducati) won	2
350cc	Norton	ET	DNF
Mallory Park, 7 September			
250cc	NSU		1
350cc	Norton		1
500cc	Norton		1
Silverstone, 13 September			
125cc	Ducati		1
250cc	NSU		1
350cc	Norton	Ignition trouble	DNF
Cadwell Park, 14 September			
250cc	NSU		1
350cc	Norton		1
500cc	Norton		DNF
Scarborough, 19–20 September			
250cc	NSU		1
350cc	Norton		1
Snetterton, 21 September			
125cc	Ducati		1
250cc	NSU		1
350cc	Norton		1
500cc	Norton	Won all four classes	1
Aintree, 27 September			
125cc	Ducati		1
250cc	NSU		3
500cc	Norton		6
Mallory Park, 28 September			
500cc	Norton	Clutch trouble	DNF
Crystal Palace, 4 October			
125cc	Mondial	First race on Mondial	1
250cc	NSU		1
350cc	Norton		1
1,000cc	500 Norton		1
Brands Hatch, 12 October			
200cc	125 Paton	Chadwick (175 MV) won	2
250cc	Mondial		1
350cc	Norton	Involved in crash	DNF
500cc	Norton		7
Inv'tion	500 Norton	Retired, ET	DNF

Race	Machine	Comment	Placing
Cape Town, Killarney, South Africa, 29 November			
250cc	NSU	Record lap	1
350cc	Norton	Equalled record lap	1
500cc	Norton	Record lap	1
Pietermaritzburg, South Africa, 14 December			
250cc	NSU	Record lap	1
350cc	Norton	Record lap	1
500cc	Norton	Record lap	1

1959

Race	Machine	Comment	Placing
Port Elizabeth 200, South Africa, 1 January			
200-m h'cap	500 Norton	Rag in carburettor	DNF
Pietermaritzburg, South Africa, 18 January			
250cc	NSU	Stander (Velocette) won	2
350cc	Norton	Chadwick (Norton) won	2
500cc	Norton	Chadwick (Norton) won	2
Mallory Park, 22 March			
250cc	Mondial	Ignition trouble	DNF
350cc	Norton		1
500cc	Norton		5
Brands Hatch, 27 March			
200cc	125 Ducati	Chadwick (196 MV) won	2
250cc	Mondial		1
350cc	Norton		5
500cc	Norton		6
1,000cc	500 Norton		3
Snetterton, 29 March			
125cc	Ducati	First win on desmo	1
250cc	Mondial		1
350cc	Norton		1
500cc	Norton	Anderson (Norton) won	2
Thruxton, 30 March			
125cc	Ducati		1
250cc	Mondial		1
350cc	Norton		1
500cc	Norton	Won all four classes	1
Silverstone, 18 April			
125cc	Ducati		1
250cc	Mondial		1
350cc	Norton	Slowed by bent valve	5
500cc	Norton		4
Mallory, 19 April			
250cc	Mondial	Gearbox trouble	DNF
350cc	Norton	ET	DNF
500cc	Norton	Anderson (Norton) won	2
Castle Combe, 25 April			
125cc	Ducati		1
250cc	Mondial		1
350cc	Norton	Minter (Norton) won	2
500cc	Norton	Minter (Norton) won	2

Race	Machine	Comment	Placing
Mallory Park, 3 May			
250cc	NSU		1
350cc	Norton		1
500cc	Norton		3
Aberdare Park, 16 May			
125cc	Ducati		1
250cc	Mondial	Crashed	DNF
350cc	Norton	Remounted to win	1
500cc	Norton		4
Aintree, 18 May			
200cc	125 Ducati	Chadwick (175 MV) won	2
250cc	Mondial	ET	DNF
350cc	Norton	ET	DNF
500cc	Norton		1
Isle of Man TT, 30 May			
F1 350cc	Norton		3
Isle of Man TT, 1 June			
350cc	Norton	ET lap 5	DNF
Isle of Man TT, 3 June			
125cc	Ducati	Clypse circuit	3
250cc	Mondial	Ignition failed leading	DNF
Isle of Man TT, 6 June			
500cc	Norton	Crashed lap 2	DNF
Mallory Park, 7 June			
250cc	Mondial		1
350cc	Norton		6
German GP, Hockenheim, 14 June			
125cc	Ducati		3
250cc	Mondial		5
Scarborough, 19–20 June			
250cc	Mondial	Record lap	1
350cc	AJS	AJS début, record lap	1
Dutch TT, Assen, 27 June			
125cc	Ducati	Led most of race	3
250cc	Mondial		4
Belgian GP, Spa, 5 July			
125cc	Ducati	Piston failed	DNF
350cc	AJS	F1 race	DNF
500cc	Norton	Machine problems	13
Castle Combe, 11 July			
125cc	Ducati		1
250cc	Mondial		1
500cc	Norton		3
Mallory Park, 12 July			
250cc	Mondial		1
350cc	AJS	Crashed	DNF
500cc	Norton		3

Race	Machine	Comment	Placing
Snetterton, 19 July			
125cc	Ducati		1
250cc	Mondial		1
350cc	AJS	Minter (Norton) won	2
500cc	Norton	Minter (Norton) won	2
Swedish GP, Kristianstad, 25–6 July			
125cc	Ducati	Rode twin-cylinder	4
250cc	Mondial		5
350cc	AJS	Lost time in pit stop	5
500cc	Matchless	F1 race	4
Oulton Park, 3 August			
125cc	Ducati		1
250cc	Mondial		1
350cc	AJS	Magneto trouble	DNF
500cc	Norton		1
Ulster GP, Dundrod, 8 August			
125cc	Ducati	First classic win	1
250cc	Mondial	Hocking (MZ) won	2
350cc	AJS	Valve spring problems	DNF
Aberdare Park, 15 August			
125cc	Ducati		1
250cc	Mondial		1
350cc	Norton	Reverted to Norton	1
500cc	Norton		1
1,000cc	500 Norton	Bike refused to start	DNF
Silverstone, 22 August			
125cc	Ducati	Won Hutchinson 100 award	1
250cc	Mondial		1
350cc	AJS	Back on AJS	3
500cc	Norton		4
Oulton Park, 29 August			
250cc	Mondial		1
350cc	AJS	McIntyre (AJS) won	2
500cc	Norton	McIntyre (Norton) won	2
Italian GP, Monza, 6 September			
125cc	Ducati		8
250cc	MZ	Début on works MZ	9
500cc	Norton	Valve gear problems	DNF
Cadwell Park, 13 September			
250cc	Mondial	Lap record	1
350cc	Norton	Reverted to Norton	1
500cc	Norton	King (Norton) won	2
Scarborough, 18–19 September			
250cc	Mondial	Carburettor trouble	DNF
350cc	AJS		1
500cc	Norton	Clutch trouble	DNF
Snetterton, 20 September			
125cc	Ducati	Record lap	1
250cc	Mondial		1
350cc	Norton		1
500cc	Norton	Record lap	1

Race	Machine	Comment	Placing
Aintree, 26 September			
125cc	Ducati		1
250cc	Mondial	Record lap	1
350cc	Norton		3
500cc	Norton	Puncture	DNF
H'cap	350 Norton	100-mile (161km) race	5
Mallory Park, 27 September			
250cc	Mondial		1
350cc	Norton	McIntyre (AJS) won	2
500cc	Norton		3
Race of Year	500 Norton		3
Biggin Hill, 4 October			
200cc	125 Ducati		1
250cc	Mondial		1
350cc	AJS		1
1,000cc	500 Norton		1
Inv'tion	500 Norton	Won five main events	1
Brands Hatch, 11 October			
250cc	Mondial		1
350cc	AJS	Minter (Norton) won	2
500cc	Norton		1
Inv'tion	500 Norton	Minter (Norton) won	2

1960

Race	Machine	Comment	Placing
Silverstone, 9 April			
125cc	Ducati		1
250cc	Ducati	World début desmo twin	1
350cc	AJS	McIntyre (AJS) won	2
500cc	Norton	McIntyre (Norton) won	2
Brands Hatch, 15 April			
200cc	125 Ducati	Record lap	1
250cc	Ducati	Record lap	1
350cc	AJS	Minter (Norton) won	2
500cc	Norton	Minter (Norton) won	2
1,000cc	500 Norton	Minter (Norton) won	2
Snetterton, 17 April			
125cc	Ducati		1
250cc	Ducati		1
Oulton Park, 18 April			
125cc	Ducati		1
250cc	Ducati	Record lap, crashed	DNF
Castle Combe, 23 April			
125cc	Ducati		1
250cc	Mondial	Reverted to Mondial	1
350cc	AJS	Record lap	1
500cc	Norton		3
Aberdare Park, 30 April			
125cc	Ducati		1
250cc	Mondial		1
350cc	AJS	Crashed disputing lead	DNF
500cc	Norton		1

Race	Machine	Comment	Placing
Mallory Park, 1 May			
250cc	Mondial		1
350cc	AJS	Retired leading, ignition problems	DNF
500cc	Norton	Record lap	1
Scarborough, 6–7 May			
250cc	Mondial		1
350cc	AJS		1
500cc	Norton	Shepherd (Matchless) won	2
Aintree, 14 May			
150cc	125 Ducati		1
250cc	Mondial		1
350cc	AJS		1
500cc	Norton	Read (Norton) won	2
Brands Hatch, 15 May			
150cc	125 Ducati		1
250cc	Mondial		1
350cc	AJS		1
500cc	Norton	Read (Norton) won	2
Silverstone, 28 May			
125cc	Ducati		1
250cc	Ducati		1
350cc	AJS	ET	DNF
500cc	Norton	Record lap, 100.16mph (161.16kph)	1
Isle of Man TT, 13 June			
125cc	Ducati	Crashed first lap	DNF
250cc	Ducati	Broken throttle cable	DNF
Isle of Man TT, 15 June			
350cc	AJS	Carburettor trouble	DNF
Isle of Man TT, 17 June			
500cc	Norton	Beaten only by MVs	3
Mallory Park, 19 June			
250cc	Mondial		1
350cc	AJS		1
500cc	Norton	McIntyre (Norton) won	2
Dutch TT, Assen, 25 June			
125cc	Ducati		8
250cc	Mondial		5
500cc	Norton	Slowed by ET	5
Belgian GP, Spa, 3 July			
125cc	Ducati	Desmo twin	6
250cc	Ducati		4
500cc	Norton		4
Brands Hatch, 9 July			
125cc	Ducati		1
250cc	Ducati		1
350cc	AJS		1
500cc	Norton		1

Race	Machine	Comment	Placing
Castle Combe, 16 July			
125cc	Ducati		1
250cc	Ducati		1
350cc	AJS	Bent valves	3
500cc	Norton		1
Mallory Park, 17 July			
250cc	Ducati		1
350cc	AJS	Valve problems	5
500cc	Norton		1
Snetterton, 24 July			
125cc	Ducati		1
250cc	Ducati		1
350cc	AJS		1
500cc	Norton	Ignition trouble	DNF
Oulton Park, 1 August			
125cc	Ducati		1
250cc	Ducati		1
350cc	AJS	ET	DNF
500cc	Norton	McIntyre (Norton) won	2
Inv'tion	500 Norton	McIntyre (Norton) won	2
Ulster Grand Prix, Dundrod, 6 August			
250cc	Ducati		4
500cc	Norton	Ignition trouble	DNF
Aberdare Park, 13 August			
350cc	AJS		1
500cc	Norton		1
1,000cc	Norton		1
Brands Hatch, 21 August			
200cc	125 Ducati		1
250cc	Mondial		1
350cc	AJS		1
500cc	Norton	Crashed, remounted	3
1,000cc	500 Norton	Minter (Norton) won	2
Snetterton, 4 September			
250cc	Ducati		1
350cc	AJS	Crashed in heat	DNS
500cc	Norton		3
Italian GP, Monza, 11 September			
250cc	Ducati	Ignition trouble	DNF
350cc	Ducati	Rear wheel collapsed	DNF
500cc	Norton	Beaten only by MVs	3
Brands Hatch, 18 September			
200cc	125 Ducati	Phillis (Honda) won	2
250cc	Mondial		1
350cc	AJS		1
500cc	Norton		1
1,000cc	Norton		1
Mallory Park, 25 September			
250cc	Mondial		1
350cc	AJS	McIntyre (Norton) won	2
500cc	Norton	Ignition trouble	DNF
Race of Year	Norton	Record lap	1

Race	Machine	Comment	Placing
Aintree, 24 September			
125cc	Ducati	Phillis (Honda) won	2
250cc	Mondial	McIntyre (Honda) won	2
350cc	AJS		3
500cc	Norton	Hartle (Norton) won	2
Oulton Park, 8 October			
500cc	Norton		5
Brands Hatch, 9 October			
200cc	125 Ducati		3
250cc	Mondial		1
350cc	AJS		1
1,000	500 Norton	Hartle (Norton) won	2
Zaragoza, Spain, 16 October			
125cc	Ducati		1
500cc	Norton		1

1961

Race	Machine	Comment	Placing
United States GP, Daytona, 12 February			
250cc	Mondial	Kitano (Honda) won	2
500cc	Norton	Ignition trouble	DNF
Brands Hatch, 31 March			
250cc	Mondial		1
350cc	AJS		1
500cc	Norton	Crashed	DNF
1,000cc	500 Norton		1
Snetterton, 2 April			
250cc	Ducati		1
350cc	AJS		1
500cc	Norton	Minter (Norton) won	2
Thruxton, 3 April			
250cc	Mondial		1
350cc	AJS		1
500cc	Norton		1
Silverstone, 8 April			
250cc	Ducati	Disqualified, having entered on a Mondial	DNF
350cc	AJS	ET	DNF
500cc	Norton	ET	DNF
Mallory Park, 9 April			
250cc	Mondial		1
350cc	AJS		3
500cc	Norton	Record lap	1
Spanish GP, Barcelona, 23 April			
125cc	EMC	Exhaust split	4
250cc	Mondial	Crashed	DNF
Brands Hatch, 30 April			
250cc	Honda	First race on Honda	1
350cc	AJS	Crashed	DNF
500cc	Norton	Crashed	DNF

Race	Machine	Comment	Placing
German GP, Hockenheim, 14 May			
125cc	EMC	Piston trouble	DNF
250cc	Honda	Rode 1960 bike	8
500cc	Norton		4
French GP, Clermont-Ferrand, 21 May			
125cc	EMC		4
250cc	Honda	Phillis (Honda) won	2
500cc	Norton		2
Castle Combe, 27 May			
250cc	Honda		1
350cc	Ducati	Won heat, did not start in final, broken frame	DNS
500cc	Norton		1
Isle of Man TT, 12 June			
125cc	Honda	First TT win	1
250cc	Honda		1
Isle of Man TT, 14 June			
350cc	AJS	Led race, gudgeon pin broke on last lap	DNF
Isle of Man TT, 16 June			
500cc	Norton	First to win three TTs in a week	1
Mallory Park, 18 June			
250cc	Mondial		3
350cc	AJS	McIntyre (AJS) won	2
500cc	Norton	Crashed	DNF
Dutch TT, Assen, 24 June			
125cc	Honda	Crashed	DNF
250cc	Honda	Record lap	1
500cc	Norton	Hocking (MV) won	2
Belgian GP, Spa, 2 July			
125cc	Honda	ET	DNF
250cc	Honda		3
500cc	Norton	Hocking (MV) won	2
Brands Hatch, 9 July			
250cc	Mondial		1
350cc	AJS		4
1,000cc	500 Norton	Crashed	DNF
Castle Combe, 15 July			
250cc	Mondial		1
350cc	Ducati	Machine problems	DNF
500cc	Norton		1
East German GP, Sachsenring, 30 July			
125cc	Honda	Ignition trouble	DNF
250cc	Honda	Record lap	1
500cc	Norton	Hocking (MV) won	2
Oulton Park, 7 August			
250cc	Honda		1
350cc	AJS	Carburettor trouble	DNF
500cc	Norton		3

Race	Machine	Comment	Placing

Ulster GP, Dundrod, 12 August

125cc	Honda		5
250cc	Honda	McIntyre (Honda) won	2
500cc	Norton	Hocking (MV) won	2

Brands Hatch, 20 August

350cc	AJS		1
500cc	Norton	Leading when exhaust broke	DNF

Aberdare Park, 26 August

350cc	AJS	Record lap	1
500cc	Norton	Record lap	1

Italian GP, Monza, 3 September

250cc	Honda	Redman (Honda) won	2
350cc	MV	Début on works MV	2
500cc	MV	First win on works MV	1

Swedish GP, Kristianstad, 17 September

250cc	Honda	Clinched World Championship	1
350cc	MV	Missed gear, bent valves	7
500cc	MV	Hocking (MV) won	2

Mallory Park, 24 September

350cc	AJS		1
500cc	Norton	Hocking (MV) won	2
Race of Year	Norton	Hocking (MV) won	2

Aintree, 30 September

250cc	Mondial		1
350cc	AJS		1
500cc	Norton		1
Inv'tion	500 Norton		1

Oulton Park, 7 October

250cc	Mondial		1
350cc	AJS	Won heat, did not start in final	DNS
500cc	Norton		1

Brands Hatch, 8 October

250cc	Mondial		1
350cc	AJS	Bike damaged at Oulton Park	DNS
500cc	Norton		3

Zaragoza, Spain, 15 October

125cc	MV	Works bike, crashed leading	DNF
500cc	MV	Won by two laps	1

Willow Springs, USA, 5 November

500cc	Norton	Record lap	1

1962

United States GP, Daytona, 4 February

500cc	Norton	Seized big-end, leading	DNF

Modena, Italy, 19 March

250cc	MV	Ignition trouble	DNF
500cc	MV		1

Mallory Park, 1 April

250cc	Benelli	Purslow's ex-works single	1
350cc	AJS	Ignition trouble	DNF
500cc	Norton		1

Silverstone, 7 April

125cc	EMC	Minter (EMC) won	2
250cc	Benelli	Redman (Honda) won	2
350cc	AJS	Minter (Norton) won	2
500cc	Norton		1

Imola, Italy, 15 April

250cc	Benelli	Ignition trouble	DNF
500cc	MV	Two pit stops to clear jets	5

Brands Hatch, 20 April

125cc	EMC		3
350cc	AJS		1
500cc	Norton	Gearbox trouble	5
1,000cc	500 Norton	Minter (650 Norton) won	2

Snetterton, 22 April

350cc	MV	British début on MV four	1
500cc	MV		1

Thruxton, 23 April

350cc	MV		1
500cc	MV		1

Austrian GP, Salzburg, 1 May

350cc	MV	Stastny (Jawa) won	2
500cc	MV	Record lap	1

Spanish GP, Barcelona, 6 May

125cc	EMC	Contested only 125cc race	4

French GP, Clermont-Ferrand, 13 May

125cc	EMC	Crashed disputing lead	DNF

Saar GP, St Wendel, West Germany, 20 May

125cc	EMC		1
500cc	MV	ET	DNF

Isle of Man TT, 4 June

250cc	Benelli	ET	DNF

Isle of Man TT, 6 June

125cc	EMC	Gearbox trouble	DNF
350cc	MV	Record lap, 101.58mph (163.44kph)	1

Isle of Man TT, 8 June

500cc	MV	Gearbox/clutch trouble	12

Mallory Park, 10 June

250cc	Benelli	Redman (Honda) won	2
350cc	MV	Record lap	1
500cc	MV	Record lap	1

Brands Hatch, 11 June

350cc	MV	Crashed, remounted	4
500cc	MV		1

Dutch TT, Assen, 30 June

125cc	EMC		5
350cc	MV	Redman (Honda) won	2
500cc	MV	Record lap	1

Belgian GP, Spa, 8 July

125cc	EMC	Cracked exhaust	4
500cc	MV		1

German GP, Solitude, 15 July

125cc	EMC	No 350 or 500 races	3

Castle Combe, 21 July

350cc	AJS	Misfire	3
500cc	Norton	Minter (Norton) won	2

Snetterton, 29 July

350cc	AJS	Engine trouble	DNF
500cc	Norton	Crashed	DNF

Oulton Park, 6 August

250cc	Benelli	ET	DNF
350cc	AJS	Minter (Norton) won	2
500cc	Norton		3

Ulster GP, Dundrod, 11 August

350cc	MV	ET	DNF
500cc	MV	Record lap	1

East German GP, Sachsenring, 19 August

250cc	MZ	Record lap	2
350cc	MV	Redman (Honda) won	2
500cc	MV	Record lap	1

Italian GP, Monza, 9 September

125cc	EMC	ET	DNF
250cc	Benelli	Crashed	DNF
500cc	MV	Clinched World Championship	1

Pretoria, Swartkops, South Africa, 24 November

350cc	AJS	Redman (Honda) won	2
500cc	Norton		1

Bulawayo, Southern Rhodesia, 2 December

350cc	AJS		4
500cc	Norton		1

East London, South Africa, 29 December

350cc	AJS	Stone hit goggles	DNF
500cc	Norton	Frame broke	DNF

Race	Machine	Comment	Placing

1963

Modena, Italy, 19 March

Race	Machine	Comment	Placing
500cc	MV	Record lap	1

Mallory Park, 31 March

250cc	Ducati		1
350cc	AJS	Blocked jet	DNF
500cc	Norton	Minter (Norton) won	2

Silverstone, 6 April

250cc	Ducati	Redman (Honda) won	2
350cc	AJS		1
500cc	Norton	Rode borrowed bike	4

Brands Hatch, 12 April

| 350cc | AJS | Crashed leading, hurt wrist | DNF |

Imola, Italy, 25 April

| 500cc | MV | Wrist problems | 3 |

Austrian GP, Salzburg, 1 May

| 250cc | MZ | Record lap, plug trouble | DNF |
| 500cc | MV | Record lap | 1 |

Isle of Man TT, 12 June

| 350cc | MV | ET | DNF |

Isle of Man TT, 14 June

| 500cc | MV | Record lap, 106.41mph (171.21kph) | 1 |

Dutch TT, Assen, 29 June

| 350cc | MV | Redman (Honda) won | 2 |
| 500cc | MV | Piston trouble | DNF |

Belgian GP, Spa, 7 July

| 500cc | MV | Record lap, 125.61mph (202.11kph) | 1 |

Ulster GP, Dundrod, 10 August

| 350cc | MV | Redman (Honda) won | 2 |
| 500cc | MV | Record lap, 101.28mph (162.96kph) | 1 |

East German GP, Sachsenring, 17–18 August

250cc	MZ	Beat Hondas	1
350cc	MV	Record lap	1
500cc	MV	Record lap, 104.72mph (168.49kph). First to win three GPs in two days	1

Finnish GP, Tampere, 1 September

| 350cc | MV | Record lap after crash | 1 |
| 500cc | MV | Record lap, clinched World Championship | 1 |

Italian GP, Monza, 15 September

| 350cc | MV | ET | DNF |
| 500cc | MV | Record lap, 119.99mph (193.06kph) | 1 |

Mallory Park, 29 September

Race	Machine	Comment	Placing
500cc	MV		1
Race of Year	MV		1

Argentine GP, Buenos Aires, 6 October

| 500cc | MV | | 1 |

Moroccan GP, Casablanca, 3 November

| 350cc | AJS | Borrowed Kirby bikes | 1 |
| 500cc | Matchless | Crashed, remounted | 7 |

1964

Daytona, USA, 2 February

Race	Machine	Comment	Placing
500cc	MV	Broke FIM one-hour World Record at 144.83mph (233.03kph)	

United States GP, Daytona, 2 February

| 500cc | MV | | 1 |

Modena, Italy, 22 March

| 500cc | MV | Crashed, remounted | 5 |

Silverstone, 7 April

| 500cc | MV | Heavy rain | 1 |

Cesenatico, Italy, 29 April

| 500cc | MV | | 1 |

Isle of Man TT, 12 June

| 500cc | MV | | 1 |

Dutch TT, Assen, 30 June

| 350cc | MV | Redman (Honda) won | 2 |
| 500cc | MV | | 1 |

Belgian GP, Spa, 5 July

| 500cc | MV | | 1 |

West German GP, Solitude, 22 July

| 500cc | MV | Clinched World Championship | 1 |

East German GP, Sachsenring, 29 July

| 250cc | MZ | Crashed while leading | DNF |
| 500cc | MV | | 1 |

Italian GP, Monza, 16 September

| 500cc | MV | | 1 |

Mallory Park, 27 September

| 500cc | MV | | 1 |
| Race of Year | MV | | 1 |

Japanese GP, Suzuka, 1 November

| 250cc | MZ | Plug trouble | 5 |
| 350cc | MZ | Rode 251cc MZ | 2 |

1965

United States GP, Daytona, 21 March

Race	Machine	Comment	Placing
500cc	MV		1

Riccione, Italy, 28 March

| 500cc | MV | Front brake trouble | 2 |

Cervinia, Italy, 11 April

| 500cc | MV | | 1 |

Brands Hatch, 16 April

| 350cc | AJS | Gearbox trouble | 11 |
| 500cc | Norton | | DNF |

Snetterton, 18 April

| 350cc | AJS | | 6 |
| 500cc | Norton | Fastest lap of day | 1 |

Imola, Italy, 19 April

| 500cc | MV | | 1 |

West German GP, Nürburgring, 24–5 April

| 350cc | MV | Agostini (MV) won | 2 |
| 500cc | MV | Record lap | 1 |

San Remo, Italy, 23 May

| 500cc | MV | Terminal misfiring | DNF |

Isle of Man TT, 16 June

| 350cc | MV | Record lap, 102.85mph (165.49kph), ET | DNF |

Isle of Man TT, 18 June

| 500cc | MV | Remounted to win | 1 |

Mallory Park, 20 June

| 500cc | MV | | 1 |

Dutch TT, Assen, 26 June

| 350cc | MV | Redman (Honda) won | 2 |
| 500cc | MV | Record lap | 1 |

Belgian GP, Spa, 4 July

| 500cc | MV | | 1 |

East German GP, Sachsenring, 18 July

| 350cc | MV | ET | DNF |
| 500cc | MV | | 1 |

Czech GP, Brno, 25 July

| 350cc | MV | ET | DNF |
| 500cc | MV | Record lap | 1 |

Silverstone, 14 August

350cc	AJS		1
Prod'n 650cc	BSA	Lightning twin	1
500cc	MV	Won on three makes	1

Italian GP, Monza, 5 September

| 350cc | MV | Record lap, crashed | DNF |
| 500cc | MV | | 1 |

Race	Machine	Comment	Placing

Mallory Park, 26 September

500cc	MV		1
Race of Year	MV	Handling problems	5

Brands Hatch, 10 October

350cc	AJS	Clutch trouble while leading	5
500cc	Matchless	Crashed while leading	DNF
Inv'tion	500 Matchless		1

Japanese GP, Suzuka, 23 October

250cc	Honda	Début on six-cylinder	1
350cc	MV	Record lap, beat Hondas	1

1966

Brands Hatch, 8 April

350cc	Honda		1
1,000cc	350 Honda		3

Snetterton, 10 April

350cc	Honda	Crashed in rain	DNF

Oulton Park, 11 April

350cc	Honda		1

Imola, Italy, 17 April

350cc	Honda		3

Cesenatico, Italy, 24 April

350cc	Honda	Provini (Benelli) won	2

Austrian GP, Salzburg, 1 May

350cc	Honda		1

Spanish GP, Barcelona, 8 May

250cc	Honda	Record lap	1

West German GP, Hockenheim, 22 May

250cc	Honda	Record lap	1
350cc	Honda	Record lap	1

French GP, Clermont-Ferrand, 29 May

250cc	Honda	Record lap	1
350cc	Honda	Record lap	1

Brands Hatch, 30 May

1,000cc	350 Honda		1

Mallory Park, June 19

350cc	Honda		1

Dutch TT, Assen, 25 June

250cc	Honda		1
350cc	Honda		1
500cc	Honda	Record lap, crashed	DNF

Belgian GP, Spa, 3 July

250cc	Honda		1
500cc	Honda	Gearbox trouble while leading	DNF

East German GP, Sachsenring, 17 July

250cc	Honda	Record lap	1
350cc	Honda	Piston failure	DNF
500cc	Honda	Broken crank	DNF

Czech GP, Brno, 24 July

250cc	Honda	Record lap	1
350cc	Honda	Record lap	1
500cc	Honda	Three wins in day	1

Finnish GP, Imatra, 7 August

250cc	Honda	Record lap	1
350cc	Honda	Record lap	1
500cc	Honda	Agostini (MV) won	2

Brands Hatch, 14 August

350cc	Honda		1
500cc	350 Honda	Gearbox trouble	DNF

Ulster GP, Dundrod, 20 August

350cc	Honda	Clinched first 350cc World Championship	1
500cc	Honda	Record lap	1

Isle of Man TT, 28 August
(Races postponed from June because of seamen's strike)

250cc	Honda	Record lap, 104.29mph (167.8kph)	1

Isle of Man TT, 31 August

125cc	Honda	Rode 5-cylinder	6
350cc	Honda	Broken valve	DNF

Isle of Man TT, 2 September

500cc	Honda	Record lap, 107.07mph (172.28kph)	1

Italian GP, Monza, 11 September

250cc	Honda	Record lap	1
500cc	Honda	Record lap, broken valves	DNF

Cadwell Park, 18 September

250cc	Honda		1
Inv'tion	250 Honda		1

Mallory Park, 25 September

Race of Year	250 Honda	Puncture while leading	DNF

Brands Hatch, 9 October

Inv'tion	250 Honda	Broken crank	DNF

1967

Mallory Park, 26 March

Inv'tion	350 Honda	Handling problems	DNP

Oulton Park, 27 March

250cc	Honda	Crashed, remounted	1
350cc	Honda		1

Cesenatico, Italy, 16 April

250cc	Honda		1
500cc	Honda	Ignition trouble	DNF

Spanish GP, Barcelona, 30 April

250cc	Honda	Puncture while leading	DNF

West German GP, Hockenheim, 7 May

250cc	Honda	Ignition trouble	DNF
350cc	297 Honda	First win on 297cc 'six'	1
500cc	Honda	Broken crank while leading	DNF

Rimini, Italy, 14 May

250cc	Honda		1
350cc	Honda	Pasolini (Benelli) won	2
500cc	Honda	Lyster frame	1

French GP, Clermont-Ferrand, 21 May

250cc	Honda	Gearbox trouble	3

Brands Hatch, 29 May

250cc	Honda		1
500cc	Honda	Lyster frame	1
750cc	250 Honda		1

Isle of Man TT, 12 June

250cc	Honda	Record lap, 104.50mph (168.14kph)	1

Isle of Man TT, 14 June

350cc	297 Honda	Record lap, 107.73mph (173.34kph)	1

Isle of Man TT, 16 June

500cc	Honda	Record lap, 108.77mph (175.01kph)	1

Mallory Park, 18 June

250cc	Honda		1
750cc	350 Honda	Valve trouble	DNF

Dutch TT, Assen, 24 June

250cc	Honda	Record lap	1
350cc	297 Honda		1
500cc	Honda	Record lap, three wins in a day	1

Belgian GP, Spa, 2 July

250cc	Honda	Ivy (Yamaha) won	2
500cc	Honda	Agostini (MV) won	2

East German GP, Sachsenring, 16 July

250cc	Honda	ET	DNF
350cc	297 Honda		1
500cc	Honda	Gearbox trouble	DNF

Czech GP, Brno, 23 July

250cc	Honda		3
350cc	297 Honda	Record lap	1
500cc	Honda	Record lap	1

Race	Machine	Comment	Placing
Finnish GP, Imatra, 6 August			
250cc	Honda		1
500cc	Honda	Aquaplaned and crashed	DNF
Brands Hatch, 13 August			
250cc 1	Honda		1
250cc 2	Honda	Record lap	1
500cc 1	297 Honda		1
500cc 2	297 Honda	Record lap	1
Ulster GP, Dundrod, 19 August			
250cc	Honda	Record lap	1
500cc	Honda	Record lap	1
Snetterton, 27 August			
250cc	Honda	Record lap	1
350cc	Honda	Record lap, ET	DNF
Oulton Park, 28 August			
250cc	Honda	Record lap	1
Italian GP, Monza, 3 September			
250cc	Honda	ET	DNF
500cc	Honda		2
Cadwell Park, 10 September			
250cc	Honda		1
350cc	297 Honda	Record lap	1
750cc	297 Honda	Record lap	1
Mallory Park, 17 September			
250cc	Honda	Record lap	1
350cc	297 Honda	Record Lap	1
Race of Year	297 Honda	Record lap	1
Canadian GP, Mosport Park, 24 September			
250cc	Honda	Record lap	1
500cc	Honda		1
Brands Hatch, 25 September			
350cc	297 Honda	Record lap	1
Race of South	297 Honda		1
Japanese GP, Fuji, 15 October			
250cc	Honda	Ignition fault	DNF
350cc	297 Honda		1
Pietermaritzburg, South Africa, 26 December			
250cc	Honda	Record lap	1

1968

Race	Machine	Comment	Placing
Cape Town, Killarney, South Africa, 14 January			
250cc	Honda	Record lap	1
Rimini, Italy, 24 March			
350cc	297 Honda		1
500cc	Honda	Reynolds frame, crashed, remounted	2

Race	Machine	Comment	Placing
Cesenatico, Italy, 7 April			
350cc	297 Honda	Crashed	DNF
500cc	Honda	Reynolds frame	2
Imola, Italy, 15 April			
350cc	297 Honda	Crashed	DNF
500cc	Honda	Reynolds frame	1
Cervia, Italy, 18 April			
350cc	297 Honda	Brake problems	3
500cc	Honda		1
Cadwell Park, 19 May			
350cc	297 Honda	Record lap	1
500cc	Honda	Wet race, handling problems	4
Mallory Park, 16 June			
350cc	297 Honda		1
1,000cc	297 Honda		1
Monte Generoso Hill Climb, Switzerland, 7 July			
250cc	Honda	Crashed, broke collarbone	DNF
Brands Hatch, 11 August			
350cc	297 Honda		1
Inv'tion	297 Honda		1
Inv'tion	297 Honda	Record lap	1
Snetterton, 1 September			
350cc	297 Honda	Record lap	1
500cc	Honda	Record lap	1
1,000cc	297 Honda	Record lap	1
Oulton Park, 2 September			
350cc	297 Honda		1
500cc	Seeley	Seeley début	1
Italian GP, Monza, 15 September			
500cc	Benelli	Crashed	DNF
Mallory Park, 22 September			
350cc	297 Honda		1
Race of Year	297 Honda		1
Riccione, Italy, 29 September			
500cc	Benelli	Gearbox problems	3
Brands Hatch, 6 October			
350cc	297 Honda	Record lap	1
1,000cc	297 Honda	Record lap	1
Pietermaritzburg, South Africa, 26 December			
350cc	297 Honda	Record lap	1

1969

Race	Machine	Comment	Placing
Cape Town, Killarney, South Africa, 11 January			
1,000cc	297 Honda		1

Race	Machine	Comment	Placing
Riccione, Italy, 30 March			
500cc	Honda	Agostini (MV) won	2
Mallory Park, 21 September			
1,000cc	500 Seeley		3
Race of Year	500 Seeley		5

1970

Race	Machine	Comment	Placing
Daytona 200, USA, 15 March			
750cc	BSA	Led race, overheated	DNF

1971

Race	Machine	Comment	Placing
Daytona 200, USA, 14 March			
750cc	BSA	Led race, valve broke	DNF
Silverstone, 22 August			
350cc	Yamaha	Borrowed works bike	4
750cc	350 Yamaha	Beaten only by 750s	4
Pesaro, Italy, 29 August			
350cc	Benelli	Agostini (MV) won	2
Mallory Park, 19 September			
350cc	Yamaha		4
Race of Year	350 Yamaha	Broken piston rings	DNF

1972–77

No motorcycle races. Banned from two-wheeled sport by car racing contracts. Won 1972 European Formula 2 Championship driving a Surtees–Ford for John Surtees. Raced for Surtees in Formula 1 in 1973. Joined McLaren for 1974 but was seriously injured mid-season in a crash at the Nürburgring. Quit racing, married, and moved to New Zealand in 1975.

1977

Race	Machine	Comment	Placing
Sydney, Amaroo Park, Australia, 23 October			
1,000cc	750 Ducati	Six-hour production machine race with Jim Scaysbrook	6

1978

Race	Machine	Comment	Placing
Bathurst, Australia, 26 March			
750cc	Yamaha	First race on TZ750, plug trouble	9

Race	Machine	Comment	Placing
Adelaide, Australia, 7 April			
1,000cc	750 Ducati	Three-hour production machine race with Jim Scaysbrook	7
Isle of Man TT, 3 June			
750cc F1 TT	Ducati	Record lap, 110.62mph (177.99kph)	1
Isle of Man TT, 5 June			
500cc	Yamaha	Steering damper broke, out of fuel last lap	28
Isle of Man TT, 7 June			
250cc	Yamaha		12
Isle of Man TT, 9 June			
1,000cc	750 Yamaha	ET first lap	DNF
Mallory Park, 11 June			
750cc	F1 Ducati		1
Donington Park, 9 July			
750cc	F1 Ducati	Crashed	DNF

Race	Machine	Comment	Placing
Silverstone, 12 August			
750cc	F1 Ducati		3
Sydney, Amaroo Park, Australia, 22 October			
1,000cc	750 Ducati	Six-hour production machine race with Jim Scaysbrook, who crashed	DNF

1979

Race	Machine	Comment	Placing
Wigram, New Zealand, 11 February			
350cc	AJS	Classic bike race	4
Adelaide, Australia, 25 March			
1,000cc	900 Honda	Three-hour production machine race with Jim Scaysbrook	14
Isle of Man TT, 2 June			
1,000cc F1	860 Ducati		5

Race	Machine	Comment	Placing
Isle of Man TT, 4 June			
500cc	Suzuki	Record lap, 114.02mph (183.46kph)	1
Isle of Man TT, 8 June			
1,000cc	500 Suzuki	A. George (998 Honda) won by 3.4 seconds	2
Mallory Park, 10 June			
1,000cc F1	Suzuki	Rode Dunstall GS1000 Suzuki, brake trouble	DNF

Index